Community Action and Organizational Change

Community
Action and
Organizational
Change

Image, Narrative, Identity

■ Brenton D. Faber

Southern Illinois University Press
Carbondale and Edwardsville

Library of Congress Cataloging-in-Publication Data

Faber, Brenton D., 1968–
    Community action and organizational change : image, narrative,
identity / Brenton D. Faber.
        p. cm.
    Includes bibliographical references and index.
    1. Organizational change. 2. Organizational change—Research.
3. Political participation. 4. Community. 5. Adjustment
(Psychology). I. Title.

HD58.8 .F3 2002
658.4'062—dc21
ISBN 0-8093-2436-9 (pbk. : alk. paper)   2001042914

CONTENTS

FIGURES

ACKNOWLEDGMENTS

Many people's stories and contributions played a significant role in creating this book. Stories do not happen in isolation. They are always community projects. For financial support throughout the early phases of this project, I am grateful to the Social Science and Humanities Research Council of Canada and for the Sherman Brown Neff Award, given by the University of Utah's Department of English.

I owe a heavy debt to those who trusted me enough to put their businesses, political campaigns, and organizations in the hands of an academic. In addition to the anonymous employees at Access Bank, MacKenzie College, and Pleasant View Cemetery, I also thank Margaret, Andrew, Neil, and Mr. Wolouski, who appear here in pseudonym but whose assistance and trust made this book possible. Thanks also go to those who read and commented on early drafts and chapters: John Ackerman, Marianne DiPaulo, Andrew Faber, Nicole Faber, Tim Garrett, Glen Hodges, Bill Karis, Frank Margonis, Art Siebert, and Sandra Zhulsdorf. Special thanks to Bill Hart-Davidson and H. L. "Buddy" Goodall for their careful, perceptive, and inspiring comments on early versions. Karl Kageff at Southern Illinois University Press stood confidently by a unique proposal and manuscript and gently helped shape it into its current manifestation.

Stephen Doheny-Farina, my colleague at Clarkson University, provided insightful advice, thoughtful comments, and unfailing support throughout this book's inceptions, drafts, and completion. For his collegiality and resourcefulness, I am grateful.

Special thanks go to Thomas and Christiane Huckin for their support, mentoring, and wisdom. Tom shares much of the credit for sparking my interest in storytelling and in writing a book that combines academic discourse with first person narrative. He has provided valuable advice along the way and remained an inspiring colleague and friend.

Most importantly, not enough thanks or praise can go to Rebecca Sutcliffe, to whom this book is dedicated, for her insights, patience, enthusiasm, and many, many stories.

Acknowledgment is made to the following for permission to reprint previously published material, which has been revised for this project: Towards a rhetoric of change: Reconstructing image and narrative in distressed organizations. *Journal of Business and Technical Communication* 12 (2): 217–37. Copyright 1998 by Sage Publications, Inc. Reprinted by permission of Sage Publications, Inc.

Community Action and Organizational Change

1 ▪ INTRODUCTION: RODEO

I know these are only words, but all the same . . . (I am moved as
though these words were uttering a reality).
　　　　　　　　　　　　　—R. Barthes, *The Pleasure of the Text*

"If it's taken a hundred years to get this far, what's another forty-
five minutes?" The summer sun has faded to a yellow and purple
glow reflecting between the clouds and the Wasatch mountains
encircling the valley. Rebecca and I are among a crowd of celebrants
waiting outside the Utah state capitol buildings for centennial year
fireworks. The show was to start at 8:00, but a rumor circulating
through the crowd suggests that we are waiting for the governor
to return from a social function. Standing shoulder to shoulder with
native Utahns, people with names like Hatch, Heber, Kimball, and
of course Young, we are interlopers. Unlike the ancestry celebrated
tonight, we flew here a mere year and a half ago when I enrolled at
the University of Utah for my graduate studies. While the Mormons'
route was west, mine was southeast, from Vancouver, British Columbia, and Rebecca, whom I met in Vancouver, eventually found
her way here after a research trip to London, England.

Our interloper status hasn't prevented us from experiencing and
enjoying Utah's centennial celebrations. For the past ten months or
so, we've been taking advantage of this centennial landmark to
explore our temporary home and surrounding state. Tonight's fireworks are a prelude to tomorrow's weekend trip to a town fair and
rodeo in central Utah. We've made it to three of these western fes-
tivals so far and have several more etched on the calendar. Despite

our attempts to pass as locals, we always miss the subtle and not so subtle signs of membership exchanged in rural America. Our jeans carry the wrong designer label and have faded too much in the wrong places; my hands aren't calloused enough; my shirt is wrong. Even with Rebecca's authentic red cowboy boots (mine are brown), we simply don't fit in.

Several days after the delayed fireworks finally dazzled above the state capitol, we are now at a very different venue. Seated along wooded planks overlooking the sandy pit of the rodeo grounds, we watch and admire the clamor of neighbors and relatives waving, talking, selling summer crafts and produce, buying hot dogs and ice cream, and rescuing children who have wandered too close to the bulls. A woman in a floral dress passes me a picnic basket. "Here, can you pass that up the line?" she implores, pointing to a group of children seated three rows above us. I pass the dinner on to a burly farmer, who finds its rightful owners. Drinks are next, followed by apple pie and ice cream for dessert.

We are seated among 250 or so fans in the stands of the town's dedicated rodeo grounds. At first glance, one would think this is a baseball diamond; however, mazes of weathered wooden rails that fence in cattle pens, horse shelters, and animal runs distinguish tonight's endeavors from solely human contests. As the boy next to me keeps repeating, mimicking a radio deejay's intonation, "Tonight, the animals get even." Like most small-town rodeos, tonight's event is the capstone of a full week's activities. Week-long exhibitions have featured the judging of local animals, vegetables, and baking. The chamber of commerce has sponsored a community merchant display in front of the school, and there has been a beauty contest to name the rodeo princess. The town's pageant is the first stage in a series of regional, statewide, and then national contests that will eventually lead to the crowning of Miss America. Today's events included a pancake breakfast, parade, and amusement rides at the fairgrounds, and tonight, the big rodeo. We left our apartment in Salt Lake at six this morning and unfortunately missed the big breakfast; however, we've hit the parade, seen the fairgrounds, lost some money throwing plastic rings at milk bottles, and now we're at the big event.

To start things off, a group of eleven cowgirls riding quarter horses gallop into the ring carrying an assortment of colored flags. They clip around the dirt stage in two opposing circles, raising the dust into a dense, choking cloud. On their final pass, they stop to form a single jagged line. Then, in what seems like a silent ritual, the men remove their hats, and the crowd stands up to greet the town's rodeo princess atop a huge white horse. She's carrying the Star-Spangled Banner, and the national anthem begins to boom through the loudspeakers. As the anthem plays, the conquering horse high-steps through the clouds of dust now settling around the ring. The princess, dressed in white, stares straight ahead, keeping a firm grip on the reins. No one waves, no one takes a picture, no one sings.

At the conclusion of the anthem, to the whoops and cheers of the crowd, all twelve women spur their horses, and the princess leads a chain of unbridled energy around and around the ring before bolting out of the arena. The dirt is phenomenal; the crowd, insane. They've come to rodeo. The loudspeakers switch to America's current Francis Scott Key, Garth Brooks, and the announcer preps the crowd for the first event, the bareback ride. The actual event is a bit anticlimactic as six of the eight cowboys get thrown early. The audience does not mind; they've settled in, passing hot dogs, beer, and soda pop back and forth along the rows. By this point, most of the teenagers have taken Daddy's money and are beginning to congregate around the competitors, trying desperately to be seen while feigning dispassionate coolness.

Between the bare backs and the saddle backs, the announcer wins the audience's attention and polite applause by announcing local birthdays. Then he directs our attention to the far end of the ring, "just above the Dodge truck sign," and asks an elderly couple to stand. "I'd like to introduce a special couple who you probably all already know." The crowd begins to hush as the announcer starts to tell us a story: "Ted and Mary Heber met each other at this rodeo fifty-five years ago today. I don't know why it took them so long, but five years later they were married, and for their honeymoon they came right back to those two seats. And folks, they've been coming back to those two rodeo seats every year for the last

3

fifty years. Let's wish them a blessed and a happy fiftieth anniversary and many, many more happy years and happy rodeos!" The crowd cheers; Ted stands up and offers a friendly wave; Mary remains seated and gently claps her hands while waving to a few friends. "In a world of constant change," the announcer booms, "it sure is nice to see that a few good things never change."

Linking Universities and Communities: The Academic Consultant

This book is about two separate but related issues: the process of organizational change and the process of researching organizational change. First, this book is about the ways people cope with change. It is about how people create change, how they adapt to change, and how they try to resist change. In other words, it is about what I call the stories of change. Second, this book is concerned with how we research and talk about change and the connections we create and sever between theory and practice, the researcher and the researched, and the academic and the community. I intentionally list these terms as binaries because they articulate an all too prevalent relationship between the university and the nonacademic community. This book will argue that such separations are rooted in everyday practices, methods, and assumptions but that we need to move beyond them in our research methods and teaching, in our ideas about universities and about community. Thus, in writing about change, this book is also an act towards change. My aims in this introduction are to discuss the approach I used to research and write about change and to orient the reader to the different projects and politics that found their home in this study.

The stories of change recorded in this book bring together a dual focus in order to talk about organizational change and simultaneously offer a model for university and community partnerships and research. In order to achieve this dual focus, I hope that this book will bring together readers interested in change both from community groups and university contexts. When referring to community readers, I look to people in business, in not-for-profit organizations, and in community action groups who are interested in a sustained examination of change. I expect that these readers want to know how to harness the power of stories as agents of change in communities and workplaces. At the same time, I look to those academic readers who want to find ways to participate more actively in, and potentially change, the communities in which they live and work. My goal is to find ways to bridge the academic/community divide, and I hope that this book initiates constructive discussions among readers who share a similar interest.

My interest in linking the academic and community emerges both from my own personal objectives and from fairly dramatic external pressures that seek to alter higher education in the twenty-first century. Put simply, North American universities are under considerable pressure to become more accountable and more relevant to the publics and constituents they represent, serve, and support. As I note in other places in this book, the critics of higher education have been sharp and sweeping in their assessment of modern schools. Stan Davis and Jim Botkin argue that "school systems, public or private, are lagging behind the transformation in learning that is evolving outside of schools, in the private sector, at both work and play, for people of all ages."[1] Donald Hanna, citing a public demand for universities to respond to adult learners, returning students, and distance learning, has argued that universities require "fundamental changes" that will involve "not just a shift in norms, structures, processes and goals, but also an essential alteration of views, perspectives, and understanding about what a university is and does."[2] Similarly, Jeanne Meister, consultant to many of America's corporate universities, portends, "Just as the American healthcare system has moved from an inefficiently managed cottage industry dominated by the public sector to a market driven system, the American educational system must now transform itself to meet consumer demands for convenient and high quality on-demand education."[3] The criticisms of higher education have not come solely from corporate America. University educator and social critic Stanley Aronowitz argues that there is little higher learning going on in the United States. By "higher learning," Aronowitz refers to "places where students are broadly and critically exposed to the legacy of Western intellectual culture and to those of the Southern Hemisphere and the East." Aronowitz further argues that as an educator, he does not wish to "reform the existing system" of higher education in America, because he is "not at all persuaded that it is possible."[4]

Thus, the stories recorded in this book emerge at a problematic time for higher education in America, and while these stories were not the direct result of any specific criticism, they did have their genesis in my own attempts to become a more engaged and community-minded academic. The stories relay a series of change-management ventures I completed as an "academic consultant," a term that will become a potentially controversial centerpiece throughout this book. In some ways, the concept of an academic consultant could be seen as heretical. Yet, like most acts of heresy, it is a stance that can also be ultimately freeing. In my own academic discipline of rhetoric and composition, academics and consultants usually are seen as two distinct species with separate goals, unique cultures, and very different worldviews.[5] Although humanities scholars have a strong tradition of social and political critique, and although we have been able to build social awareness, community building, and critique into our teaching, we have thus far been less able to form a theoretically rich tradition of research based on our community activism. It is the purpose of this book to combine the two positions of academic and community activist in order to initiate a much needed, empirical-yet-activist discourse about change and community action.

Rodeo Stories and Rodeo Culture

Ted sits back down and shares a quick kiss with Mary. The crowd settles in for more rodeo action as the bulldoggers warm up their horses by doing short sprints in the grass behind the south side cattle pen. It's an odd sight: waves of four and five horses and riders accelerating away from the two ambulances, fire truck, and nearby beer tent and public outhouses. One might think some cowboy terrorist organization has just bombed the concession booth. Or, once the cowboys start swinging their giant lassos, it looks like waves of drunk, injured rodeo participants are trying to escape without paying their entrance fees. Rodeo is a culture of its own, and though numerous coffee table books, Hollywood fantasies, and country music songs have tried to capture the dry grit of rodeo, very few readers appreciate the cultural role rodeo manifests in hundreds of small towns across America. Rodeo is a performed memory of the past, of the days when the West was newly settled and honest people did honest work. It's a testament and reminder of the backbreaking work good families did to tame the West.

That's one story of rodeo. Of course, if you walk in the head office of PETA (People for the Ethical Treatment of Animals), they'll tell you a mighty different story, and if you ask any of the rodeo managers who direct these traveling P. T. Barnum-esque shows throughout Utah, Idaho, and Wyoming, you'll probably get yet another story. However, these different stories are so divergent, so removed, and so antithetical to each other that they have little chance of ever intersecting and an even less chance of really influencing each other. If anything, when these stories clash, they seem to only reinforce each other. For example, several months ago we decided on a whim to go see a movie at a downtown Salt Lake City movie theater. However, our plans were disrupted by a crowd of thirty-five or so rain-drenched anti-rodeo protesters standing outside the main entrance to the theater. We didn't know this, but the theater was showing the rodeo movie *8 Seconds,* the story of bull rider Lane Frost, the first person in over three hundred attempts to ride a famous bull named Red Rock. Frost and Red Rock were 1987 national rodeo champions, Frost the champion rider and Red Rock the champion bull. In the spring of 1988, Frost and Red Rock completed a seven-event playoff, seven rides at seven different rodeos. Frost won the competition, four rides to three throws. In the process, Frost became the only person to ever ride Red Rock, and he immediately became a hero among rodeo faithful. In 1989, Frost was killed by a bull named Taking Care of Business at the Cheyenne Frontier Days Rodeo. *8 Seconds* was much more than a rodeo movie; directed by John Avildsen, of *Rocky* and *Karate Kid* fame, the story canonized a fallen hero.

Finding the rodeo protesters' attempts to change the minds and attitudes of some pretty serious fans far more interesting than another evening at the movies, I stood by and watched as rural Utahns in Wranglers, cowboy boots, and hats forged their way through lines of Berkenstock-clad demonstrators who waved signs and umbrellas as they chanted slogans condemning rodeo's treatment of animals. Even the parking lot surrounding the theater illustrated the fact that these were cultures with little in common as half- and full-ton trucks competed for space with foreign station wagons, sedans, and an occasional VW bus. It was soon apparent that although the people standing in the rain genuinely wanted to change the opinions of those whose pickups were being targeted with pamphlets, leaflets, and other assorted materials, tonight they were only insulting their audience. In the minds of moviegoers who had named their kids "Lane" and "Lynette," the protesters were desecrating a culture, a history, and, more importantly, the stories they told themselves and their children. Here, change was all about stories, but because the stories were so divergent, so opposite to each other, there was no possibility that either side was about to change. Instead, those in each group simply reinforced the other group's stories and perceptions held of their opponents. No one had created or presented a larger story to pull these people together; there was no common narrative they could both embrace. As a consequence, without a unifying story, one that spoke to both groups, neither side was about to change.

From Ethnographer to Activist

This book was conceptualized initially as a series of mini-ethnographies about change. These were going to be qualitative studies of changing workplace cultures I would conduct by immersing myself in a workplace's everyday activities, daily conversations, mundane texts, and familiar routines and then watching how these tokens of the everyday were influenced by various change management initiatives. And for the most part, this project's first study, an examination of change at a financial institution, unfolded as it should have. I initiated that study as a graduate student at the University of Utah, and I fully intended to complete a fairly typical ethnography of organizational change. However, throughout the research and the reporting that emerged from this research process, I became somewhat frustrated by my academic positioning. Even though I had attempted to fully immerse myself within my research context, I was still an academic observing and reporting events as

I witnessed them. My subjects knew this, and although they were informative and understanding, they knew that I had no actual stake in the situation I was observing. As my research continued, I found that my position as "observer of change" was too isolated and too protected. Studying change solely as a researcher did not provide me with the kinds of risks or responsibilities I needed to fully understand and fully experience the processes and the risks of change.

John Van Maanen has characterized alternative ways of collecting, interpreting, and reporting ethnographic data as "confessional" or "impressionist" ethnographies.[6] For Van Maanen, confessional tales are highly personalized accounts that focus as much on the researcher's own learning and experience as they explain or reveal information about the subject of the research. Such an approach is usually undertaken as a response to the researcher's discovery that the expectations of objective research do not hold. The confessing researcher realizes that subjects do not give unbiased accountings of their experience, that the environment under examination overtly changes when the researcher appears, or that the researcher has self-consciously become emotionally involved or otherwise "contaminated" by the research.[7] In response to this crisis of objectivity, the field-worker decides to "confess" and reveal himself or herself as an active participant in the process of discovery, interpretation, and reporting.

This confessional results in a report that is part autobiography and part empirical report. Although the writer is self-consciously implicated in the process of research, this does not take away from the adequacy or the reliability of the work. In fact, many would argue that a confessional tale is more reliable because the author is clearly present on the page and does not need to obscure difficult findings, irreconcilable accounts, or subjective interpretations behind a cloudy but nevertheless thin veil of objectivity.

Van Maanen describes "impressionist" tales as startling, striking, active tales of research as discovery, shock, and expression.[8] Impressionist tales are often dramatic and engaging. As Van Maanen writes, "The intention is not to tell readers what to think of an experience but to show them the experience from beginning to end and thus draw them immediately into the story to work out its problems and puzzles as they unfold."[9] Impressionist accounts are less concerned with presenting a coherent argument than with displaying a vibrant picture or complex scene, immersing the reader in the details of the activity. Ideally, an impressionist ethnography will provide what Van Maanen calls a "you-are-there" feeling, a sense that the reader can actually witness and learn from the events as they occur.[10]

The accounts that follow in the chapters of this book borrow much from both confessional and impressionist ethnography. However, for Van Maanen and other ethnographers, the process of research remains a process of observation rather than action, of witnessing rather than doing. Of course, there are exceptions. For example, Ralph Cintron notes that in the process of researching his ethnography *Angels' Town,* he was an active member of several community organizations, participated on a school board committee and a city-sponsored task force, tutored children, wrote official letters for his subjects, and acted as a translator.[11] As Cintron notes about his own work, research frequently begins as an extension of activism. Nancy Scheper-Hughes, in an often cited passage from her ethnography *Death Without Weeping,* describes her own positioning as a qualitative researcher:

> On the day before my departure in 1982, a fight broke out among Irene Lopes and several women waiting outside the crèche where I was conducting interviews and gathering reproductive histories. When I emerged to see what the commotion was about, the women were ready to turn their anger against me. Why had I refused to work with them when they had been so willing to work with me? Didn't I care about them personally anymore, their lives, their suffering, their struggle? Why was I so passive, so indifferent, so resigned? . . . The women gave me an ultimatum: the next time I came back to the Alto I would have to "be" with them—"accompany them" was the expression they used—in their "luta" and not just "sit idly by" taking field notes. "What is this anthropology anyway to us?" they taunted.[12]

Similarly, Carl Herndl and Cynthia Nahrwold have suggested an alternative way to conceptualize academic research and activism. They argue that a researcher's purpose is not shaped as much by methodology as by social awareness and social activism. Herndl and Nahrwold write: "Whereas most scholars writing about qualitative research assume that a researcher's 'purpose is shaped by epistemological and methodological commitments,' we argue that the reverse is true. We suggest that a researcher's commitments to specific forms of social action shape theoretical and philosophical commitments."[13] Herndl and Nahrwold articulate a continuum of research practices that suggest that most research is ultimately political in that it can be focused on maintaining social orders, describing social orders, or changing social orders. Academic work inspired to change social orders assumes that teachers, students, and researchers have a responsibility to challenge oppressive practices and work towards the elimination of inequity and the construction of positive social change.[14]

I agree with Herndl and Nahrwold that considerable research in the humanities and social sciences has political motivations, and yet, all too often, ethnographic work reports on a struggling community, a workplace literacy program, or a workplace experiencing radical cultural change without showing the engagements between the researchers and those being studied. This does not mean that ethnographers have merely "sat idly by taking field notes" while people struggle. In fact, as the example above from Cintron's book demonstrates, many good ethnographers are motivated by their own activism and attachments within the communities they study. At the same time, this deeper connection often goes unreported in ethnographic studies. Such an omission is ironic since the rich details and close analysis inherent in ethnographic work often lead to direct political significance and important policy implications. But, despite the fact that academics have advanced degrees, access to significant intellectual and material resources, flexible schedules, and daily contact with bright, idealistic, and challenging students, the conventions of academic reportage rarely allow public activism to be freely admitted or profiled as an essential part of the research enterprise. Unfortunately, academic work is still based on observation and description rather than engagement and activity.

H. L. Goodall has attempted to reconfigure this descriptive posture of a traditional ethnographer when he describes what he calls an "organizational detective," one who is part scholar, part detective. As I became increasingly frustrated with more passive forms of data collection, I found myself turning towards Goodall's hybrid who "enters into the culture of organizations armed with a sense of mystery, an attitude of healthy skepticism, . . . a respect for the dignity of ordinary people, and a duty to report as fully and as completely as possible the details of the case."[15]

What attracted me to this model was that it presented a researcher who fully investigates the research site but is not afraid to engage the research as a critic, consultant, and, in my own case, as a community activist. Given that qualitative research is often highly personal, I think there were also more personal, storied reasons why I wanted to adopt a more hands-on approach to my research. In the early 1950s, my grandfather Dirk Faber was building himself a home in a growing immigrant community outside Hamilton, Ontario, Canada. A few blocks away, a contractor was building a dormer out the front of a house. These were the days before contractors used trusses or prebuilt dormers. Dirk was intrigued by this new architectural design and stopped by one day after work in the steel ovens at Stelco, Hamilton's largest steel mill. "How do you do that?" he asked the contractor, who laughed and said something like, "Dutch, if you want one of these, you'll have to find yourself a good architect and then wait in line." Not to be swayed, Dirk made a point of stopping by the work site every night to watch the roof's progress. A week later, he wasn't satisfied with what he was learning. Simply watching the builders work was not teaching him the intricacies of the design, the way the beams were cut, the angles of the roof line. So, late in the week, he stopped after the contractor's crew had left for a neighborhood pub. Dirk reached into the back of his car and pulled out a hammer, a crowbar, and a pencil. He climbed up to the top of the nearly-finished dormer and took the entire structure apart. Then, scribbling the dimensions, cuts, and angles down on the back of a cigarette package, he put the whole thing back together again. A month later, he built a dormer on the front of his house. As Goodall notes about his organizational detective, this is "a professional snoop, a social philosopher, and a comic actor, a person who is street-wise and willing to do what needs to be done."[16] Like my grandfather before me, after concluding my observation-based research, I took out my hammer, crowbar, and pencil and decided to become a self-conscious participant within my own studies of change.

I found that in order to fully understand change, I needed to play a self-conscious, direct role in change and fully experience the consequences, successes, and risks associated with change. I felt that unless I had a real stake in the projects I undertook, I could never claim to have a deep appreciation for change. Unless I could feel the very real risks associated with change, I could not legitimately write about change. At the same time, I was inspired by the potential of forming academic and community alliances and by situating qualitative research within active community work.

For these reasons, I adopted the dual position of an academic consultant. This was a difficult position to occupy. As a consultant, I became an expert who was paid to supply expertise and implement solutions. Unlike a "pure" researcher, my time was not my own, but I was accountable to my clients. This had a significant impact on the time and resources I could spend on participant observation, surveys, focus groups, interviews, or other forms of data gathering. Although I completed many of these tasks, my research was constantly constrained (and questioned) by time, client deadlines, and client expectations. For most of the time I conducted these studies, I did not have a formal university position. I conducted the research for chapter 2 as a graduate student at the University of Utah, but the other chapters were conducted as a self-employed consultant. During this point in the research process, I was dependent on my work as a consultant and on my wife's income as an assistant professor. My business model was to work with nonprofit groups on change-management issues. As I was dealing with a relatively impoverished clientele, my business model was modest. I was not going to get rich, but I tried to remain self-sufficient and use as little family resources as possible in maintaining my practice.

At the same time, during the two and a half years of this research, I remained a member of my academic discipline, reading and publishing articles in academic journals and attending academic conferences. I remained active at my local university, working as a curriculum consultant helping faculty implement communication projects within courses, leading a project team that designed an endowed chair position in engineering communications, and, for one term, teaching a course in technical writing for the engineering school. Throughout my research, I was up-front about my dual status. I asked my subjects/clients' for permission to observe what they were doing and to freely publish the results of my work. In all cases, I have changed people's names and the names of their work sites to retain their privacy and anonymity.

A word about the style of this book: *Community Action and Organizational Change* is not only about the roles stories play as agents of change, but most of the chapters, with the exception of chapter 1, take place as a series of stories. My intent here is to present these stories of change in much the same way actual stories of change appear within the organizational contexts I studied. The point here is that such stories may not appear to hold the methodological certainty most academic readers anticipate; however, these stories still play powerful and significant roles within personal and organizational contexts. In addition, within these contexts, people make pivotal, life-changing decisions without the kind of certainty my professional academic culture often stipulates. These professional forces have unfortunately created an artificial, yet hierarchical, divide between what is considered "research" and what is condemned "a story." This division has provided academics with a perhaps necessary but somewhat luxurious, and even envious, decision-making environment. Academics are able to postpone action until we are absolutely sure our information is correct. However, outside of the academy, people need to make decisions in less than ideal environments. In the face of change, people need to act. This book works from the premise that when given partial information and little time, but facing actual implications and real consequences, people rely on quick, inconclusive, surface readings of the stories they see happening around them. These readings are partial and flawed, but, as Roland Barthes notes in the quotation I used to open this chapter, "All the same, they are moving."[17] Some readers may find sections of this book overly academic; others may find chapters too popular or storied. I ask those readers to keep in mind the book's larger goals and to remember that bridges are only useful when they unite two (or more) separate landscapes.

Rodeo Revisioned

Thinking back to Ted and Mary, the rodeo couple who seemed to have escaped change, I have often wondered if there were other stories to tell about them—not stories about how they have resisted change over the past fifty years but how they have embraced and created change. If there were such stories, I bet they would go something like this:

"Well, we'd better get a move-on if we're going to catch the rodeo this year." Ted slides back from the dinner table, surveying the devastation they have jointly brought to another anniversary meal of baby back ribs, scalloped potatoes, peas, and squash. Mary doesn't care much for the squash, but it's a perennial favorite of Ted's, so she doesn't mind it on special occasions.

"You load up the dishwasher while I fix my hair," Mary shouts en route up the stairs. Despite the routine of this ceremony, Ted can't help but admire the efficiency of the dishwasher with its spaces for plates, bowls, big cups, glass cups, and cutlery and a long narrow basket that perfectly holds the chopsticks he and Mary get with their Chinese food from the strip mall in town. Ted remembers when that place first opened up. "We didn't think it would last much past Friday, being in cattle country and all." But Mary insisted they try it out, and despite himself, he's been volunteering to "get take out," as they call it, most Saturday nights. "It provides jobs for local farmers," Ted tells himself, so he mostly orders the beef dishes to accompany his spring rolls and hot and sour soup. He always puts the wooden chopsticks in the narrow basket of the dishwasher, and once they are clean he places them in a ceramic container next to Mary's bread maker. He had saved quite a collection up until last year when Mary gave them to their granddaughter's church school class. The first graders were studying Noah, and each child was going to build an ark for racing in the spring run-off from the nearby mountains. Unfortunately, arks were a little too technically advanced for most, so the failed arks became Moses baskets and the spring run-off, the Nile.

Ted always feels conspicuous driving to the rodeo in a sedan. He'd much rather be in his pickup, but several years ago he hurt his back shingling the porch roof. Actually, he injured himself falling off the porch roof, but he doesn't tell anyone that. The pickup seemed to aggravate the injury, so he traded it in for a used Oldsmobile. Truthfully, he prefers the ride, the comfort, and the spaciousness of the Olds, especially when he and Mary head up to Salt Lake to visit their grandchildren. But it's tough for an old rancher to be without his truck. In some ways he realizes this is a rite of passage, and he reasons that it's good to have a vehicle Mary is comfortable driving, just in case anything happens, of course. As well, this way they can put their two grandkids in the back—something they could not do with the truck. To prove his point, Ted had two child seats installed in the back a week after buying the car. He now tells the younger guys at church that he and Mary just might start all over again.

Ted parks the Olds a few rows away from the entrance to the rodeo arena. There was a closer parking spot, but it was beside a bright green foreign car. "Probably one of those animal rights people," Ted thinks as he walks by the car. He recalled a newspaper story about animal rights activists protesting a Lane Frost movie in Salt Lake. Ted was at that Cheyenne rodeo, and he watched helplessly as Frost collapsed in the ring. Though he's been watching bull riders for nearly all his life, and though he even found himself getting thrown off an occasional bull back when he worked on his grandfather's ranch, after Cheyenne he could never sit still during a bull ride. But Ted wasn't the only one who had changed over the years; the rodeo had changed too. Ted often wondered if new technology had made some of the guys a bit loose with the stock. He and Mary had the president of the local town rodeo over for dinner several years ago when the stock hands first used cattle prods to jump-start an animal. Ted told him that the stock had been bucking fine without that added incentive. In his day, all you needed to control your stock was a good horse and a good dog. The president thanked Ted and Mary for the meat loaf and mashed potatoes and said he would take their concern "under advisement."

Looking around, Ted is still surprised at how different the rodeo has become. He first started bronc riding as an eight-year-old on his father's ranch. There, the rodeo was a way to practice skills and break in the stock before the summer's run. Then, other ranches started having competitions among their cowboys to see who could rope the best, who could ride the fastest, who could outlast the ranch's toughest bull. Now, Ted knows that few of the competitors work ranch life. He knows about the rodeo schools, the training camps, the big time management, and the ways rodeo has become big business. He's disappointed when there are no local guys to cheer for and when the barrel racers are from places like Texas, California, Missouri, or Canada. It's as if two different stories are going through his head. On the one hand, he identifies with the story about the old rodeo, about local kids testing their strength and testing their animal stock. On the other hand, he knows the story about developing the West, about bringing money to these deserts they call towns, about leaving something behind for the next generation who will try to scrape a living off of this land. Yet, as he watches the first four cowboys get thrown off their bareback mounts, he has yet to reconcile the two accounts.

Mary grabs his hand as the announcer starts reading off birthdays. He'd almost forgotten that they were told about a special welcome they would be getting at tonight's event, it being their fiftieth and all. Ted looks over at a delighted Mary, brimming in the glow of her anticipated fifteen seconds. He met Mary at this rodeo fifty-five years ago. He was riding a bull and she was barrel racing. He got thrown and she won. That was the year she went all the way to the state finals. Oddly enough, he hadn't really noticed her until that night when he saw her straining the horse around the last barrel and down to the home stretch. He never told her, but just as his bull was being let loose—with him holding on for dear life—her red vest caught his eye. He looked one way, the bull looked the other, and he hit the ground, breaking three ribs and an ankle. Worst use of an entry fee he ever squandered. For a while, he wondered if there could have been an easier way to meet her. But, he's never regretted the fact that he did.

"Ladies and gentlemen, if I could direct your attention to the far end of the ring, just above the Dodge truck sign," a voice booms over the loudspeaker. "Ted and Mary Heber met each other at this rodeo fifty-five years ago today. I don't know why it took them so long, but five years later they were married, and for their honeymoon they came right back to those two seats. And folks, they've been coming back to those two rodeo seats every year for the last fifty years. Let's wish them a blessed and a happy fiftieth anniversary and many, many more happy years and happy rodeos!" The crowd cheers; Ted stands up and offers a friendly wave; Mary remains seated and gently claps her hands while waving to a few friends. Sitting down beside her, Ted gives Mary a quick kiss on the cheek. Over the booming voice of the announcer, Ted whispers in her ear, "I'm sure glad we do this every year. It gives me a chance to see just how much life around here's changed."

2 ▪ READING THE STORIES OF CHANGE

Familiar though his name may be to us, the storyteller in his living immediacy is by no means a present force. He is already becoming something remote from us and something that is even more distant.
—W. Benjamin, "The Storyteller"

Stories of Change

Carefully cross-stepping around—and inevitably through—the slushy mixture of snow, sand, and salt, I am tacking across the last major street before my afternoon run takes me along a stream of wooded trails flowing out of the city. Once across the street, I will pick up the gravel trail that winds through a series of forested buffers, wooded lots that isolate the city's suburban communities from each other. At the five-mile mark, I will reach Chicopee Ski Club, a series of moderate ski hills just outside of the city's reach, where most of my neighbors learned to ski before they moved on to more extreme adventures in New York, Vermont, or Montreal. After climbing the back side of Chicopee, my route descends to the main lodge, the summer tennis courts, and a small pond before the potholes of a little-used back road would return me to the city.

Although I had not run this course in the ten years since I moved away, this was a familiar route. I began logging miles here when I started running nearly twenty years ago. When I was eleven years old, these trees coached me through my first six-miler, and runs up and down the ski hills prepared me for my first marathon. College and graduate school took me away to explore other trails and test different hills. But now, returning to this route, I am enjoying this reacquaintance with my boyhood haunts: remembering the familiarity of the trail, reexperiencing the haunting darkness of the forest and the flush of its birds, and feeling again that intimate strain of each hill. Passing around Chicopee's pond and returning to snowy pavement, I experience again, perhaps for the hundredth, hundredth time, regret for losing the trail but relief for nearing an exhausting end. From this point, I will climb one last hill before a gradual four-mile downhill slope carries me home.

A few hundred yards along the road, I come to a full stop. There is no hill. In fact, there is no road. The road I am following curves to the right and enters a subdivision where a cornfield was supposed to be. Where I expect to see my familiar route rise to a grove of trees and a few dilapidated houses, a grass boulevard crests away from a bright white sidewalk to a chain-link fence. Through the fence I can see an intersection complete with streetlights, and beyond that, a neighborhood of detached homes. I stumble to the top of the median, grasp the fence, and stand watching the sea of garages, kitchens, fire hydrants, sewers, bus stops, children playing street hockey, and parents unloading groceries from their minivans. This is another world, a suburban universe that has displaced the rural familiarity of my forgotten road, the lines of crab apple trees, the rambling yellow house perched at the top of the hill, the grove of cedar trees midway down the slope, the memory of home. I am suddenly very cold and very tired. Things are different, and I am unable to comprehend this difference. I have nothing to communicate, no stories, no messages, nowhere to go. In the face of change, I am lost.

What role do stories play in contexts of change? Why do people tell stories about work, about family, about community? What kind of stories are these, and what do these stories achieve? Are stories simply the products of change, or might stories have a more powerful, more compelling function as agents of change? Could we say that our stories actually construct change?

Roger Rosenblatt, whose essays regularly appear on *The News Hour with Jim Lehrer,* chose to discuss the social purpose of stories in his final news essay of the twentieth century. In his "Millennium Essay" read December 31, 1999, Rosenblatt writes:

In the final days of the Warsaw ghetto, the Jews imprisoned there had no doubt that they were going to die. They had seen others taken away to the extermination camps, and they were dying on their own of starvation and disease. Still, in those last days, the people wrote stories: Fragments of autobiography, diary entries, poems, letters, accounts of events. They wrote them on scraps of paper and rolled them into the crevices of the walls of the ghetto. They knew they were done for. They felt certain that the Nazis had taken over the world; that if their little writings were ever discovered, it would be by the Nazis, who would laugh at their puny efforts and toss the scraps of paper away. Why did they do it? Why bother to tell a story that no one would hear? And why make the telling of that story their last act on earth? Because it is in us to do so, like a biological fact—because storytelling is what the human species does, to progress, to learn to live with one another. Horses run, beavers build dams; people tell stories.[1]

This book argues that change itself is a story, and stories are acts of change. The stories we read, watch, hear, create, and enact are powerful, interpretive acts. They provide security and continuity. They create resistance, opposition, and conflict. They provide a cultural record of who we are, where we have been, and what we hope to achieve. Stories document our habits, successes, failures, and lessons learned. They place our culture's defining events, oddest moments, and strategic messages into common narratives we assimilate, refine, and then pass on to next generations. In the process, we add to these stories different expressions, subtle distinctions, and small deviations. We leave out details we believe are unimportant, information we forget, and issues we would rather not remember. We suppress competing voices, conflicting dogma. And, all the while, we narrate change.

Stories are an intricate part of our personal and professional lives. As Rosenblatt later notes, a law trial is "a competition of stories," and businesses use stories to make money: "Stories of former successes and failures direct decisions to buy, sell, merge, expand, downsize, go public." In medicine, stories dominate human practices as the patient tells the doctor a story, then the doctor responds with another. As Rosenblatt states, "The doctor tells the patient this will happen and that will happen, until, one hopes, the story has a happy ending."[2] The stories we tell interpret and create meaning out of the changes we experience.

I recently spent a week at an international management consulting company's training center. As part of my research there, I had the opportunity to watch a class of junior managers who were learning how to present "value statements" to the firm's clients. These consultants were learning how to tell a client that the work the firm was completing had real economic value. This is a more difficult task than it might seem. Although the high-powered experts can see immediately how their work can benefit a client, the employees who are comfortable with their positions, the managers who like the familiarity of the company's routines, and the contented executives who are satisfied with the company's performance need to be persuaded that there are good reasons to pay a group of consultants considerable sums of money to turn their workplaces upside down.

The course I observed was structured as an "educational immersion," meaning the students worked together in teams on a simulated business project. One course instructor—Jasper, a retired senior executive—role-played the client, a vice president at Secure Corp., a fictitious national insurance company. A second instructor—one of the firm's senior partners—role-played the supervising partner. Two other instructors worked as team coaches. The course positioned the students as a team of "replacement consultants" who were brought in to fix a project that had gone awry at Secure Corp. Using course materials, the students were required to assess the client's situation, uncover the business problem, and then recommend and implement a business change process. The case places the students in a problematic and diplomatic situation because they are told that the preceding group of consultants made little progress over their fourteen months at Secure Corp.

From the course's opening session to its conclusion five days later, it is an intense experience. There is no "downtime" during the simulation. Even when the teams took Jasper out for lunch or when they accidentally met at the local mall, Jasper remained in character, pressing the consultants on time-lines, services, and value. According to the simulation, Jasper's character had already dealt with one team of unsuccessful consultants and had become considerably impatient with this project. "This is nice," he would reply after the students presented their results after a day of intensive number crunching, "but why should I do it and what value does it add to my company?"

Early on, the students had a difficult time relating to Jasper. Presentations flopped, plans seemed unclear, analyses were off the mark, and the teams were becoming increasingly frustrated. After a particularly uneventful student meeting, I stopped by Jasper's office, and we discussed the students' difficulties. Jasper told me that he was not surprised that the students were not connecting with him yet. He noted that these students were still relatively inexperienced consultants who had spent the past five years learning the firm's values, priorities, and systems. At this point in their careers, they were used to communicating with each other and with other firm employees. However, as they advanced in their careers and took on more supervisory positions within the firm, these consultants needed to look beyond their own organizational culture and learn how to read their clients. Unless they took the time to learn their clients' priorities, histories, and values, Jasper argued, these consultants would not be able to effectively communicate with their clients.

I thought about Jasper's comments, and I remembered a video the class had watched on the very first day of the course. This was a professionally produced news magazine, based on the sort of exposés one sees on 60 Minutes. The video included interviews with the current CEO of Secure Corp., past and present executives, and industry experts who provided commentary and insights into Secure Corp. and the insurance industry. The video revealed that Secure Corp. recently endured a period of poor decision making that had resulted in three years of net losses, a shrinking customer base, negative press, and dwindling public opinion. However, throughout the video, the executive who spoke on behalf of Secure Corp. was self-confident, positive, and dogmatically unrepentant. He discussed a few broad issues but did not suggest that the company was in crisis.

According to the CEO, the previous team did not understand the company's key messages or the internal and external risks faced by Secure Corp. The executive is a master of slight of voice; in his discussion he leaves many things unsaid but clearly implies that he is not happy with the advice he had received and would like to cancel this project. In summing up his experience so far, the CEO turns to the camera and says, "I am just a small-town boy from Iowa; my father told me not to jump into a river until I could tell how deep it is." The implication is that the consultants want to build a tire swing, but Secure Corp. still is not sure it remembers how to swim.

The next day, I sat down with Jasper and told him the following story:

> Secure Corp. has its roots as a small-town, conservative firm from Iowa. Back then, it knew how to judge risk, how to tell when the river was just right—how to find the deep spots and avoid the shallow runs. But since those days, the company has grown and it has changed. Now, it serves people in cities and states its founders had never even visited. As a result, Secure Corp. has lost its ability to measure the depth of the river. Sometimes it jumps; other times it just stays on the bank—not because it can't swim but because it doesn't know whether or not it is going to kill itself or sink to the bottom.
>
> We are going to take Secure Corp. back to that river bank in Iowa, and we are going to teach you not just how to measure the water's depth but how to measure the current, how to look out for sharp objects, and how you can teach other people how to judge these risks too. We'll even provide life guarding and swimming lessons so you can adapt to times when the river changes.

Jasper folded his hands and nodded, "That's a good story; now you've got my attention." He and I then talked about corporate stories and how these stories bring meaning to the company and the ways they can teach astute consultants about their clients' cultures. Jasper said that in the rare occasion when a consultant actually learned, repeated, and then used his company's story, he could see that this external expert had taken the time to understand his company. He argued that too many consultants, like the students I had been watching, were focused solely on the numbers and were unable to put these numbers into a broader and more meaningful context. "Of course," Jasper grinned, "I would still expect your numbers to add up, or you'll be out on the street with the rest of them." But Jasper agreed that what differentiates the good consultants from the bad are those who take the time to read, learn, and integrate a company's stories before they start telling people what to do and how to change.

All I had done in my conversation with Jasper is repeat back to him the stories his (fictional) boss was telling. Secure Corp.'s CEO was using the familiar story of an Iowa swimming hole as a metaphor to talk about his company's culture, about the ways it manages and undertakes risk, and about the values it holds. The insurance industry is all about managing risk and, like a young boy standing beside a river, it needs to be able to assess risk versus profit. The team of student consultants missed the significant message this simple story told. They jumped too quickly to the meanings, the numbers, and the details without first considering the story.

Toward a Theory of Change

This book suggests that stories broker change because they mediate between social structures and individual agency. In other words, stories help us negotiate between those factors that restrict and limit our possibilities and our free ability to pursue our own choices. This duality is present because stories take place as discursive (or language-based) events, and it is these events that are at the heart of change. Throughout this book, I will be arguing that change is inherently a discursive project. This means that change is restricted by the structures of language and by the conventions of language use. Change will be a product of what can be legitimately said (or written) in a specific context at a specific moment in time. At the same time, change grants us new forms of agency and offers new choices and options.

The idea that change can be restricted or held back by something as simple as language may seem paradoxical. In most cases, we think of change as a radical alteration of current reality—a decisive break from what we know and what we experience. But, this phenomenon of difference (that things are no longer the way they were) is only one aspect or moment of change. It is the spark that puts the process of change into motion. Actual change is as much a process of reconciliation or reconstitution as it is a process of differentiation. Too often, we confuse difference with change, not realizing that change is a much richer, dynamic concept. Change is a process of reconciling the differences we experience in our daily lives. Simply acknowledging or recognizing that the world is suddenly different is not enough. True change reconciles that difference and reforms it, making it part of our everyday lives.

This book argues that processes of change have five key constituting features: identity, communication, narratives and images, discordance, and reconstitution. In what follows, I will briefly summarize this framework, demonstrating how the book's chapters elaborate and develop this discursive model of change. I see this model as descriptive as it is prescriptive, meaning it can be used as a way to interpret change and as a way to plan and manage change.

Identity

Change is primarily a function of identity, and, thus, issues of identity inform each of the following chapters. Identity is closely linked to communities and to cultures as it is an interpretation and a performance of our cultures and our cultural stories. Change enables the members of an organization to successfully restructure and reposition their own identities—and their larger organization's identity—as they strive to resolve their competing needs, expectations, and goals for the organization.

Gibson Burrell and Gareth Morgan write that the concept of organizational culture was developed as an extension of anthropological studies associated with Malinowski and Radcliffe-Brown.[3] This anthropological research developed a functional analysis of culture that investigated unusual or special events within social systems. For example, a church community can be said to have a distinct local culture that is created through the church's many functions: baptisms, worship services, marriages, funerals, church school, and the other things the church's members do that distinguish their group as a unique community. These social functions are networks and relations that provide continuity across the community. Thus, the term "culture," according to this perspective, loosely identifies regularized, performed functions that hold a group of people together.

This consideration of workplace culture is evident in Michael Hyman's recollection of experiences within the burgeoning computer industry of the 1980s.[4] Hyman recalls working for Microsoft when it and IBM joined forces to produce a PC operating system.

Despite being the decade's two leaders in the computer industry, Microsoft, with no dress code, few restrictions on employee conduct, and few security protocols, operated as the cultural antithesis to a staid IBM, which required all employees to wear white shirts, implemented strict policies regarding employee conduct, and used security passes in all corporate buildings. Hyman reports that while working at IBM, Microsoft employees often took full advantage of these two companies' different cultural practices at the expense of IBM:

> IBM had a very strict policy on keeping documents secure. Confidential documents could only be sent back and forth to Microsoft using certain approved carriers. Thus, if a programmer visited IBM for a technical meeting, he couldn't take back any IBM specifications with him on the airplane. The specs had to be sent by separate courier, even if the programmer was carrying a Microsoft version of the same document. At one point, we planned to photocopy the title page of a spec (which just said "IBM Confidential") and leave it around at various points at the airport nearest to IBM's Boca Raton offices.[5]

On another occasion, Hyman reports that all visitors at IBM had to be escorted at all times. IBM would reprimand and even fire employees who let visitors walk freely around the hallways. When visiting IBM, groups of Microsoft employees would often threaten to run in different directions.[6]

These accounts are insightful for their portrayal of the intersection of two very different organizational cultures and for their demonstration of the ways in which employees identify with or against organizational cultures. Robert Heath argues that organizational culture influences behavior "because it contains the social reality people use to know what they are expected to do." This cultural knowledge defines what is appropriate and what is not, and as Heath asserts, it enables people to "coordinate their efforts" and socialize themselves as part of the organization.[7] As such, this adoption of cultural norms can be seen to be a process of interpreting an organizational identity and then shaping one's own identity as a part of the larger construct within the organization.

Organizational identity—the visible, performed interpretation of organizational culture—should be seen as a highly contested terrain during times of change. The term "organizational identity" points to those signifiers that enable people within organizations to situate themselves as distinct from those working in other organizations. This identity is performed in the ways people dress, the cars they drive, the architecture and interior design of an organization, and the communicative genres people use within the organization. For example, when launching their new PC-based operating system in 1995, Microsoft strategically integrated the identity of their product with the identity of Microsoft the organization, launching an innovative and somewhat raucous campaign, which included hanging a multistoried banner on Toronto's CN Tower; placing a full-page ad in the *London Times,* purchasing the day's entire newspaper run, and then giving away copies of the paper; and launching the product at midnight to assure lineups at stores and maximum press coverage.

Microsoft's campaign relied heavily on its emerging identity as a fresh, radical, upstart player within the computer industry and within popular culture, and it used this identity to distinguish its products from its competition. A Microsoft employee who was involved with the launch of this operating system informed me that for the first few months after the product launch, Microsoft employees would give away promotional gifts (shirts, software, certificates) to computer store staff who answered telephone calls by repeating a Microsoft slogan.

Despite the successful connections Microsoft forged between its product and its identity, these identities are not fixed or stable. As Norman Fairclough has argued, identity should also be seen as a strategic and situational response to particular needs at particular times.[8] For example, when Microsoft defended itself against federal accusations of unfair trading practices, it took on a considerably different identity than it did when it launched its operating system. Yet, given the important connections between workplace culture, which inundates all aspects of organizational life, and organizational identity, which performs that culture, the processes whereby an organization strategically adopts a new identity should be seen as a highly complex, intricately managed, and highly problematic task. This is the function of organizational change: to affect the deeply rooted cultures of an organization by using stories to alter the organization's visible signs of those cultures, its identity.

Communication

Change, as an identity function, occurs as a communicative project. This means that change occurs through the manipulation of specialized forms of language. More often than not, the primary form of this communication is storytelling. This finding is grounded in observations of organizational life that have shown the powerful roles communication plays in creating and maintaining organizational structures.[9] Organizational communication enables business processes, constructs organizational knowledge, and creates the everyday workplace stories that make it possible for people to work together.

This important connection between communication processes and organizational change is elaborated in chapter 3, which reports on change-management initiatives conducted by Access Bank, a financial services company located in the American West. Access wanted to reinvigorate the bank and improve sagging revenues by moving a greater portion of deposit income (the money customers place in savings and checking accounts) to its recently established investment division. The investment division would invest this money in stocks, bonds, mutual funds, and other forms of "alternative investments," thereby aspiring for greater returns on customers' accounts and assuring higher revenues and greater investment capital for Access.

A major obstacle challenging this new direction was the fact that few current employees at Access were aware of the investment market, no members of the bank staff were licensed to sell these products, and many of the long-term bankers had grown comfortable in a banking culture. In order to alter deep-rooted cultural antagonism towards investment products, Access's training programs were designed to educate staff about these new investment products and socialize the bankers into a new investment-oriented culture at the bank. This new culture created new stories at the bank that told of bankers successfully pursuing new clients, working hard to service customers' needs, growing their branches' revenues, and gaining early promotions and bonuses by referring existing clients to the investment division.

Embedded within the story of Access Bank is the start of a more theoretical discussion that simultaneously weaves its way through this book. These breaks in the chapters' larger narratives raise more complex issues associated with organizational change. For example, chapter 3 introduces the idea that much of what people believe and do comes from unconscious decisions, habits, and routines. Because of the prominent role these unquestioned routines play in our lives, we are more likely to resist change because it can force us to reconsider those things we have always just assumed. These assumptions and beliefs create real structures in our lives. These are social, spiritual, and material structures that provide meaning, identity, and coherence but at the same time restrict agency, expression, and freedom.

But, this is not the place to fully revisit this discussion. Instead, I hope to simply foreshadow these successive discussions and note that they were designed to build on each other, chapter by chapter, as a companion to the book's larger stories. I should also forewarn that the story about Access ends on a more distressing note. When I returned to Access several months after my first round of data collection, I found out that many of my subjects (the students in the change-management courses I observed) had been forced into early retirement or were simply fired as the bank tried to more radically change its culture. In discussing these events with my contact at Access, the point was raised that although I witnessed the bank's changes and saw how they were trying to implement change, I, as an outsider from the relatively stable world of the university, could not really know or understand these changes because I was not experiencing them the ways the people at Access were. I thought about this accusation for some time, as it made me reconsider my relationship with Access and the people I studied there. I conclude the story of Access by questioning the ways my work there benefited the population I studied. In short, the chapter examines my own discourse of academic researcher and finds it somewhat lacking. This discussion then introduces the book's critique of passive research and sets up the more activist agenda profiled in chapters 4, 5, and 6.

Narrative and Image

An organization's identity takes shape in two complementary forms: organizational narrative and organizational image. Narratives are constructed internally as a manifestation of "insiderness" within the organization. Images are constructed externally by competitors, clients, customers, and other interested groups. At any point in time, an organization's identity is reflected in the convergence of its narratives and images. The stories people tell about change occur in this intersection between narrative and image. Although the term "narrative" is often used interchangeably with the term "story," I am using narrative to refer to a smaller but necessary component of stories. Stories of change are products of identity, communication, narratives and images, discordance, and realignment. As such, they are about much more than narratives. However, narratives do play an essential, constitutive role within the story.

Narrative. The concept of organizational narrative is not new to communication scholarship. Dennis Mumby has noted that narrative is "a socially symbolic act in the double sense that (a) it takes on meaning only in a social context and (b) it plays a role in the construction of that social context."[10] Mumby argues that narrative constructs a "site of meaning" in which "social actors are implicated." In other words, narratives are contextual products that both construct an interpretation of an organization and situate social actors within that construct. As such, Mumby notes that narratives are not stable and fixed but are part of a "complex and shifting terrain of meaning."[11]

Further, Mumby argues that narratives enable groups of workers to frame the interests, needs, and perspectives of other groups within the organization. Here, narrative acts as an instrument of power within organizations as predominant narratives structure how people view their organizational environment. As such, Mumby argues that narratives "constitute the organizational consciousness" of groups of workers, and they can "articulate a form of social reality" that is accepted by most members of the organization.[12]

Robert Heath describes organizational narratives as the stories and presentations people tell at work as a way of explaining "why we do things we do." As Heath writes, these stories "give insights into how people enact and recall relationships and policies as episodes—details of organizational activities and opinions."[13] Narratives play an important role as an interface between an organization's cultures and its identity. Members of an organization learn the firm's cultures and develop an identity as part of the organization through the firm's narratives. As Anthony Kerby has shown, narrative "is a question of what, in reflection, we make of our situation vis-à-vis the past, present, and future."[14] In this way, a narrative stands in for, or represents, our experiences, and it enables us to construct an identity within these experiences.

Shortly after I completed my work with Access, my wife, Rebecca, and I moved north so that she could begin teaching at a Canadian university. As she taught, I began working on various community projects as an "academic consultant." Chapters 4, 5, and 6 emerge from these experiences and detail my attempts to actively create change within these organizational and community contexts.

Chapter 4 narrates a story of organizational change at MacKenzie College's program in massage therapy. When I was approached by Neil, the director of the program, the internal relations at MacKenzie were a mess. Students were rebelling against teachers, teachers were suspicious of the students, and no one could get along with the school's administration. The chapter argues that the program and the school itself did not have a clear narrative that presented its mission, goals, and policies. As a result, students and teachers created their own institutional narratives, which only created more trouble for the school. I was brought in to write an organizational text that could restore relationships within the school and help turn the institution around. The chapter asserts the importance of a central narrative to the function of an organization and argues that these narratives require constant maintenance and revision. At MacKenzie, I learned that if an organization does not invest in maintaining and telling its narratives, others will tell these narratives instead—and one can never predict what kind of tales others might tell.

As a significant device for constructing both organizational and personal identity, narratives emerge from within organizational discourse and build credibility because they are a part of this discourse. Narratives are part of what Berkenkotter and Huckin have identified as "insider knowledge" within an organization.[15] Narratives utilize terminology and vocabulary that is unique to the organization. They highlight the actions of specific individuals and charismatic leaders and refer to important organizational events or occasions. Through this insider knowledge, narratives denote what Pierre Bourdieu calls the symbolic capital of the community, the markers that denote importance and belonging within a specific group.[16] In other words, narratives are internal constructions that distinguish and politicize what members of an organization value. At the same time, these narratives denote the various identities members claim and provide the framework from within which new members may choose their own organizational identity.

As a theoretical discussion, chapter 4 develops the concepts of narrative, structure, and organizational change through a presentation of the "operations of structure." Here, the chapter revisits the agency/structure debate by forwarding various notions of structure and the vital roles structure plays in organizational life. This discussion argues that in their desire to embrace acts of agency and resistance, many theorists too quickly dismiss structure and often miss the important nuances and complexities embedded within organizational and social structures. This is not to suggest that structure is all-encompassing but rather that is it often overlooked or underestimated as a social and political force.

Image. If organizational narratives denote the structural ways an organization's insiders view the organization, organizational image denotes how interested outsiders view the organization.[17] As described by Gareth Morgan, image is "part of the self-referential process through which an organization attempts to tie down and reproduce its identity."[18] Images exist apart from the organization as something it often attempts to assume but not as something it absolutely controls. Morgan suggests that organizations recognize their image by looking to their environment and creating a picture of themselves within this environment. In this way, an organization's image derives from indicators of the organization's position within its environment, its sales records, market analysis, customer demands, consumer boycotts, government actions, and so forth. All of these indicators are a mirror that reflects the organization's image back onto itself.

This definition of organizational image is similar to that developed by Catherine Casey, who suggests that an organization's image can derive from a combination of corporate name, products, employees, marketing strategies, and the ways in which the organization describes itself within the larger marketplace.[19] Even though the ways in which an organization describes itself often influence the production of its image, an image may be created in opposition to an organization's discourse or in the absence of such discourse. This is often the case when external groups launch campaigns against a specific product or company, as evidenced by the repeated campaigns against Nike's labor practices. Although Nike has attempted to control the projection of its image through newspaper advertisements and specialty web pages, other groups have attempted to alter this image through their own publicity and alternative web pages.[20] This ongoing campaign demonstrates that image is often more temporal than organizational narrative and that image can often become a struggle between many competing and uncontrollable forces.

Chapter 5, "Image: Power, Rhetoric, and Change," tells the story of an election campaign in northern Canada. Here, I was involved as part of a grassroots undertaking to nominate a friend, Margaret, to be our candidate in an upcoming election. Americans would call this a primary; Canadians, a nomination campaign. Elections represent a fundamental way in which regular citizens can work for change at both local and national levels, and this campaign was no different. Margaret would be the region's first female candidate, and her platform emphasized fiscal responsibility, job creation, entrepreneurship, and accountability. Yet, although this was a story of change, it was also a story of power and image, because Margaret hoped to defeat a consummate party insider who had a strong local image supported by his family connections, social status, and political connections in the community. As we soon discovered, and as this story details, an image is dynamic; it competes, interacts, supports, and supplants other competing images. And, through these contests, groups outside of our organizations or communities will form images of who we are and how we act. In the case of Margaret's campaign, we found that the projection of her image was directly connected to issues of power and change within the community. We soon learned that a successful reading of change must also include a strategic and sophisticated reading of image and power.

Organizational image can be seen to be a component of corporate ethos. As a rhetorical term deriving from the three ways in which a speaker secures persuasion, ethos is usually associated with the character and virtuous nature of the speaker.[21] Similarly, Roger Cherry has argued that ethos "refers to the need for rhetors to portray . . . good moral character, practical wisdom, and a concern for the audience."[22] As Cherry shows, ethos enables a speaker to gain credibility with an audience; however, as Gary Hatch notes, this credibility is gained only insofar as the audience is willing to concede it. Hatch writes that ethos derives externally, "based on how others perceive" and not entirely on how the speaker would want to be perceived.[23] In the same way, an organization's image is constructed and held by the audiences of its communication and derives from more sources than just the organization's own communication. This image is an important reflection of how the marketplace views the organization, how customers perceive products, and from where potential difficulties, boycotts, campaigns, or customer dissatisfaction may emerge. At the same time, image is an always vulnerable location that can undermine and destroy even the most credible speakers.

The story of Margaret ultimately argues that contests of image and contests of change are really contests of power. However, whereas power has traditionally been seen as a top-down phenomenon in which the powerful dominate the powerless, the chapter argues that power should instead be conceptualized as a much more dynamic, productive, and insidious phenomenon. Viewing power as an exclusively oppressive phenomenon does little to characterize the multiple ways in which power operates. In addition, seeing power only as overt expression does not allow us to see power in its more common and more influential operations. For example, the chapter argues that power is embedded in acts of resistance, it is responsible for obscuring ideologies as "natural" or "normal" expressions, and it is about reproducing itself in silent and unacknowledged ways. By examining issues of agency and resistance through the lens of power, we can see that power is about one's self-reflexive ability to control an image. Powerful organizations and people are able to influence the ways in which others view them. Organizations that are powerless have no control over the ways people view and interpret them.

Discordance

Organizations become distressed when their externally projected images conflict with their internally produced narratives. This conflict results in discordant and potentially damaging organizational identities and organizational stories.

This component of change emerges most dramatically in chapter 6, which reports on my work at Pleasant View Cemetery. "Discordance and Realignment: Stories from the Final Frontier" relates my experience writing a five-year business plan for Pleasant View, a city-owned cemetery. A cemetery is not what usually jumps to mind when one thinks about organizations and change-management. However, I found this to be a fascinating challenge: How does one create change within an institution based on absolute permanence and certainty? The study examines the cemetery as an organization and traces the many stories that I found throughout my time there.

While researching what would become Pleasant View's business plan, I realized that the cemetery, as an organization, was caught between two very different perspectives of itself. On the one hand, employees at the cemetery could narrate the vital role this organization plays within the city. To them, the cemetery preserved and promoted a vital link with the past; it accommodated and thereby fostered diverse religious and cultural practices; its streets, lined with over a thousand trees, memorialized soldiers who died in battle; and its thick, dusty book of records maintained a vital record of settlement in the area. On the other hand, many of my city's politicians did not even know that the city owned a cemetery. The city's chief bureaucrat became interested in the cemetery only when he suddenly needed to make funeral arrangements for his mother. To make matters worse, a multinational corporation approached the city with an offer to purchase the cemetery for $2 million. With the offer of money on the table, the cemetery's image suddenly became numerically defined, and city leaders saw the cemetery in terms of money: revenues, expenses, break-even pricing, and possible net worth. Many politicians openly wondered what they could purchase with the money gained from selling the cemetery.

This case demonstrates the often drastic ways in which an organization's narrative may diverge from or contradict its image. Even though the cemetery had a well-defined and healthy internal narrative, few people outside of the organization shared or recognized this story. As such, this narrative was openly contradicted by the image most people had of the cemetery. This narrative/image contradiction was evident in declining business (a growing number of people were choosing to be buried in a new for-profit cemetery), internal problems among the cemetery staff, a stagnant organizational climate that had no plans for meeting new trends in the industry (cremation, natural settings, prestige locations), and the possible corporate takeover of the organization.

To argue that change is sparked by a contradiction in the narratives and the images of an organization may seem to oppose various postmodern theories that assert the heterogeneity of identity and the ability of subjects to often retain two (or more) contradictory identities. For example, Lawrence Grossberg refers to the construction of "plural identities which are never fixed and never settle into a fixed pattern." Grossberg and others argue that subjects participate, identify, and form identities in diverse and often contradictory communities. According to this view, subjects often hold contradictory identities and may switch from one to another given situational need and exigence.[24]

Fairclough employs a different perspective on this issue of contradictory identities, suggesting that such contradictions are "likely to be manifested experientially in a sense of confusion or uncertainty" and as such will most likely lead to substantive change within the subject.[25] My own research supports Fairclough's claim. The divergent identities pulling at the cemetery were causing a great deal of organizational distress and uncertainty. This was also the case at Access Bank and with Margaret's election campaign. At Access, the bank's new narratives recalled great customer service, pioneering product development, and historic leadership, but the bank's image reflected an out-of-date, rigid institution that was unwilling to consider consumer demands or alternative approaches to banking. This image of a stale and unchanging bank was projected in financial magazine articles about the bank, and it was repeated often in interviews I conducted with competing banks and investment houses. Margaret and her supporters thought her political campaign was about making the political system more representative and more participatory; however, the image she projected was of an outsider who wanted to take power away from the long-standing members of the community. Interestingly, the issue at MacKenzie College was somewhat different. At MacKenzie, the school's image was of a friendly, empowering organization that took care of its students and its patients. However, the narratives that emerged from within MacKenzie contradicted this image. These stories told about abusive teachers, unsympathetic administrators, and a classroom climate that was hostile and embarrassing. In each of these cases, the organization's images contrasted and in some cases openly ridiculed the organization's narratives. This became the crisis that led to each organization's change.

As the story of Pleasant View Cemetery unfolds, chapter 6 simultaneously turns to a different kind of discord by investigating many of the assumptions common in ethnographic and observation-based social research, like the research conducted for this book. Working from Bourdieu's critique of social science, the chapter suggests that objective, disinterested perspectives actually create a distortion in social analysis because what emerges from such research is not the everyday working knowledge of members of the social group but a distorted representation of this knowledge. Bourdieu argues that the problem with much social analysis is that it is formed without practical ability or competence in the research area. The result of this work is an academic's rendition of an issue or context and not a representation of the practical work and the necessary day-to-day aspects of life within that context.

Realignment

The book's final chapter is about realignment. Here, I argue that organizational change is the communicative process of realigning the organization's discordant narratives and images. It also realigns the book's sometimes diverging components as it brings together its theoretical, narrative, and observational currents. As it builds this realignment, the final chapter presents practical ways in which universities, community groups, and businesses can come together to create spaces for practice, experience, and action-based learning and social research.

I argue in the chapter that change can be a stabilizing and re-cursive force as an organization's stories pull discordant images and narratives back into a sense of temporary alignment. This final component of change may appear antithetical to established notions of change, since change is rarely associated with unity, continuity, or agreement. This has certainly become the case in an organizational climate that has associated change with downsizing, right-sizing, restructuring, and other forms of layoffs and cutbacks. However, as Michael Hammer and Steven Stanton write, these processes of downsizing have largely resulted in organizational failures. Hammer and Stanton describe downsizing as simply "an act of desperation—throwing people overboard to lighten the financial load."[26] Robert Johansen and Robert Swigart argue that the most significant results of organizational downsizing are the excision of organizational memory, the destruction of employee motivation and loyalty, and the erosion or elimination of communication networks throughout the organization.[27] Even Robert Tomasko, whose book *Downsizing* links change management with reducing employees, eliminating managerial levels, and cutting budgets, has admitted that the original model has not been practically successful. In his 1993 book, *Rethinking the Corporation,* Tomasko writes that "more than half the 135 major U.S. companies that attempted massive restructuring failed to achieve significant increases in their value relative to their competition." Tomasko further writes that of one thousand midsized companies that attempted to change through downsizing, fewer than half actually reduced expenses, only 22 percent made improvements in productivity, only 25 percent attained desired cash flow or share values, and only 15 percent reduced bureaucracy and sped up decision making.[28] Interestingly, Tomasko's newest book is titled *Go for Growth!: Five Paths to Profit and Success—Choose the Right One for You and Your Company*. Chapter 1 is titled "Build, Don't Destroy."[29]

As a conclusion, chapter 7 takes this theory of realignment back to the book's discussion of higher education. In it, I bring together the different layers of this book by discussing ways academics and community groups can create positive change. First, I introduce the concept of identity-stories, which are the perceptions of ourselves we gain from the stories around us, then contend that the identity-story of the university is being subsumed by interests outside of the university: corporate interests, government interests, and market interests. In order to reestablish the university's identity story, I argue that scholars within universities need to better link their research and teaching interests with community needs and civic projects. In conclusion, I articulate three ways for such partnerships to occur: service learning courses, action research, and nondisciplinary writing.

As mentioned above, this book asserts that a distinction can be made between the concepts "difference" and "change." Organizations can be made different through restructuring, reducing work forces, and eliminating managerial layers, but these differences do not necessarily create change. Difference is a process of elimination, discordance, and disparity; it is the spark that reveals contradictions between narrative and image. Change, on the other hand, is the process that restores stability to the distressed organization. This means that change is perhaps most importantly an act of persuasion. Unless advocates of change can convince others that the organization is actually distressed, there will be no need to reach a new state of equilibrium. Similarly, if a distressed community, organization, or person is unwilling to take on a new identity, change cannot happen.

Heath's concept of change also asserts an important re-constitutive function. Heath writes that change "requires that the company become, in terms of actions taken and rewarded, what it wants to be perceived to be and how it wants employees to behave."[30] When integrated with a model of change that emphasizes restoring discordant narratives and images, Heath's description articulates an ongoing process whereby organizations continually monitor and address the gaps between their narratives and their images. Thus, difference should be seen as a momentary and temporal stagnation that prevents the ongoing maintenance and realignment of narrative and image. Simply replacing employees, eliminating divisions, or firing large numbers of staff is not only unlikely to make a significant change in the distressed organization but also may actually prevent the organization from reconstituting its distressed identity. As Heath writes: "Changing employees—firing many and hiring others—is unlikely to change the company unless the culture also changes. The employees who remain keep stories alive and pass them along to new employees who may enact the culture that existed before the turnover. The 'massive turnover of 1985' merely becomes part of the narrative of the culture and adds evidence for a negative view of the company."[31] As such, forcing difference onto an organization, through downsizing, prevents that organization from strategically changing. This occurs because these processes falsely promise change without addressing those factors that produced the narrative/image disparity and prevented the organization from continuously acting to reform and reconstitute its narrative and image.

However, as the chapters that follow will show, change must be situated within current discursive practices—even if it hopes to alter or deny those same practices. Otherwise, change loses credibility and becomes an act of violence, repression, or censorship. While language restricts change, it simultaneously frees it, giving change voice and agency. Thus, the stories that construct change provide both the discursive structure and agency necessary for successful action and for successful change.

Stories of Communities and Organizational Change

The stories that make up this book are my own readings of change. They take place in settings that are highly volatile and interpretable. They discuss attempts to create change and attempts to resist change. Some of the stories are tales of success; others are tales of failure. However, in each case, the story presents an accounting of change and a thick description of the activities involved in reading and writing these changes. A careful reader will see that these stories are also somewhat autobiographical, and I hope that they demonstrate some of the ways I have experienced change as I, simultaneously, have been change's student.

By working through various stories of change, the book narrates several different ways stories construct, maintain, and ultimately change organizations and the people who work there. The book presents stories that engage change at both a large, organizational level and at an intimate, personal level. Within an organization, stories play essential roles in socializing employees, creating efficient processes across the corporation, formalizing an organization's memory, and carrying and projecting a organization's image both inside and outside the organization. An organization unaware of its stories is unaware of its identity and, as such, risks having its identity formed by competitors, regulators, or other hostile forces.

However, an organization keenly aware of its stories can use them to make both minor daily changes and more radical significant changes throughout the organization. For this reason, stories are vital to any type of change because an organization's stories help to align its internal and external identities. Stories merge the ways people inside and outside the organization perceive and describe their interpretation of the organization. As evidenced throughout the chapters in this book, a strong story can influence the ways an organization is perceived, especially in times of duress or confusion when a dysfunctional organization must reconnect with its central mission and objectives.

At the personal level, the book suspects that people rely on stories to create their own personal identities and their images of themselves. Whether read from religious texts, popular culture, literature, family lore, classical mythology, or one's calculus teacher, stories provide us with the images we use to construct our own identities. Through these stories, people create new identities, strengthen existing identities, or critique and evaluate their own and others' identities.

But before we can move on to the stories of change, readers must realize that every organizational story was written to achieve an end, every tale told to persuade its audience to think or behave in a specific way. Thus, when encountering organizational stories, we need to ask a few questions: Who wrote this story? What does the story hope to accomplish? What do I need to believe in order to buy this story? Who profits from this story? Who loses in this story? Can I accept the consequences of the story? Before accepting or rejecting organizational stories, it is important to understand the power relations that endorse the story, the social work the story accomplishes, and the ultimate consequences of the story. Too often, we accept organizational stories without engaging these stories for their political, ideological, and value-based judgments. We must learn to read the story as a conduit for a certain, selective way of viewing the world.

What do we gain from reading change as a story? A good story, suitably barbed, will work itself deep into memory. But reading our stories—the stories of our organizations, our communities, and ourselves—loosens their quills, denaturalizes their power, and reveals their influence and their interest. When these barbs are finally removed, we can begin again to write change.

3 ▪ TIME, HABITS, AND CHANGE: BROKERS, BANKERS, AND THE OLD WEST

In 1848, James Marshall discovered gold on the South Fork of the
    American River.
In 1984, America's banks discovered the stock market.
In 1996, I discovered Penny's.

Change and the American West

Western writer Larry McMurtry has noted that America's western
experience has "demonstrated perhaps more clearly than any other
the astonishing speed with which things change."[1] Citing the mere
twenty years it took to render nearly extinct fifty million buffalo
and the half-a-cowboy's-lifetime in which the vast expanses of
Montana, Wyoming, Utah, and Colorado were partitioned and
fenced, McMurtry shows that stories of the American West are
fundamentally stories of change. Or, alternatively, they are stories
about coming to terms with change.

   In much the same way as the railway, the cowboy, the immigrant, and the discovery of gold transformed the American West,
the stock market, the credit card, and the rise of corporate finance
has transformed the American banking industry. This transformation was not an easy task. But most observers of the American
banking industry in the mid-1980s and early 1990 would have said
that such a task was necessary and perhaps overdue. Throughout
the 1960s, 1970s and early 1980s, bankers, with conservative financial products, long-term, no-risk approaches to money manage-

ment, and a community-based public ethos, largely appeared as the antithesis of the short-term, high-risk, quasi-ethical personae of Wall Street stockbrokers. Indeed, from the period of 1933, marked by the passing of the Glass-Steagall Act, to the banking crisis of the mid-1980s, commercial banking was largely a passive, highly regulated, and highly repetitive business wherein banks made money by charging higher interest for loans and credit than they paid in savings and checking accounts.

The culture that emerged from these practices was as standardized and traditional as the products the banks offered. Bank operations, often described as "white-collar factories" or "public utilities," focused on following fixed procedures, fostering long-term customers, minimizing risk, and avoiding change. Banking was a lasting, usually lifelong, employment, and it provided a comfortable, secure standard of living through salaried wages and regularized increases based on longevity with the company. As David Rogers notes, the culture attracted (and recruited) affluent but mediocre Ivy League graduates who reproduced the predominantly white, Anglo-Saxon, Protestant management and who functioned well within a bureaucratic, regulation-bound environment.[2] Rogers writes: "Little emphasis was placed on developing new products or on the aggressive marketing of existing ones. The protected market of the commercial banks didn't require such an emphasis and there were no rewards for it. Salaries were not high, because there was no need to attract the most talented people."[3]

As banks continued to foster relatively complacent financial practices, several new companies and organizations were establishing a beachhead on the banks' traditional territory. One of the first and perhaps the most successful company to offer competing financial products and services was Sears Roebuck and Company. Financial analyst Cleveland Christophe showed that in the early 1970s, Sears's after-tax income from its financial services was greater than the income of any U.S. banking organization, and this income accounted for a third of Sears's net earnings.[4] Peter Rose has shown that, during the 1970s, Sears Roebuck offered a wide range of products and services, including personal financing, insurance, sales of mutual funds, business management, investment consulting, residential housing construction, and mortgages, in addition to a travel bureau and automobile club. At this time, the volume of actively used Sears credit cards exceeded Americans' combined total use of both VISA and MasterCard.[5]

Sears's success was complemented by a variety of other non-bank participants in America's financial services industry. Companies like American Express, General Motors, and Merrill Lynch, in addition to credit unions, money market mutual funds, and an increasing number of retail chains, manufacturing companies, and industrial companies, offered consumer loans, sold interest-bearing products, issued consumer credit, and maintained personal consumer accounts. Whereas large companies would previously turn to banks for loans or credit, they could now issue bonds or investment certificates to raise money apart from America's banking establishment.

This development seriously undermined a bank's ability to retain deposit accounts and generate income. The Glass-Steagall Act of 1933 required banks to separate all securities affiliates from commercial banking, a policy that effectively removed banks from the securities business, and it was only in 1961 that most banks began to offer interest-bearing accounts.[6] As more knowledgeable consumers realized that they could achieve better returns from non-banking products, more and more money left the banks in favor of alternative investment plans. In the twenty-four months from 1979 to 1981, Merrill Lynch's money market accounts built up fund balances that exceeded the total domestic deposits that America's largest bank (Citibank) had acquired over 160 years of operation.[7]

This movement of money away from the banks, combined with the phenomenal success of money market mutual funds and securities investments, led to a decade of crisis for American banks. In 1980, nine of the ten largest savings banks in New York City reported net operating losses totaling $264 million. In 1983, forty-eight American banks failed; in 1984, seventy-nine banks failed; and in the first ten months of October 1985, ninety-five banks failed across the county. As an editorial in the December 27 *New York Times* argued, 1984 was the most tumultuous year in the history of banking in America.[8]

In response to this erupting financial crisis and the continuing erosion of consumer confidence in the banking industry, the federal government, from the period 1984 to 1986, authorized what has now come to be known as the "deregulation" of the American banking industry. The two most significant policies to emerge from this legislation were the enabling of large banks to operate branches in more than one state and the enabling of bank holding companies to engage in securities trading, apparently leveling the ground between the banks and America's large investment houses.

For roughly two years, I had the opportunity to study and watch one of America's top ten banks attempt to change itself into a more dynamic financial services company. For reasons of confidentiality, I'll call the bank "Access" and note that the branches I followed were located in the American West. Access's current incarnation was created by a merger between the old Access Bank and Esquire Bank (also a pseudonym), an elite bank catering to upper-income, highly educated customers and blue-chip corporations. Prior to its merger with Esquire, Access was one of the fifty largest banks in America. One analyst, writing in *Business Week,* described Access as the "Wal-Mart" of banks, as it catered largely to smaller population areas and boasted "relationship banking" within those communities.[9] In addition, between 1987 and 1990, Access took full advantage of the deregulation of state borders and tripled its size by purchasing branches across America.

Analysts saw the merger with Esquire as an awkward but convenient marriage, since Access had developed a large network of branches in small-town America and close ties with small business, farming, and individual customers, whereas Esquire had fewer branches but an extensive investment management portfolio and a strong background in trust services and corporate finance. The resulting company emerged as one of America's ten largest banks and was well positioned to place investment banking and "alternative investments" in most small towns and larger cities across America.

Despite the promise of increased market share and improved revenues, two years after the merger, Access's profits had fallen 3 percent, and the bank's stock had not kept pace with stock values of equivalent banks. In an interview with *Forbes* magazine, the vice president of community banking for Access suggested that the bank's poor performance was attributable to the bank's underappreciation of the "obsolescence" of the branch banking system. The vice president reported that Access needed to "change the behavior of the community bank" by changing how people working in local branches thought about their everyday jobs.

Access's plan to revitalize its branches took two directions. First, Access wanted to invest in new technology that would help branch staff better target new customers and help cross-sell products to existing customers. The idea here is that if customers have at least two products with the bank—a car loan and a savings account, for example—they are more likely to turn to that same bank when they need a credit card, a home mortgage, or, in this case, stocks, bonds, and mutual funds. Second, Access planned to turn branch employees into energetic salespeople, radically changing the traditional role of a bank employee. The new plan envisioned bank managers spending 50 to 75 percent of their time on the street, meeting new customers, cold-calling potential clients, and creating relationships throughout the business community. Rather than sitting behind a desk and waiting to reject the next loan application, these bankers would be actively selling loans, mutual funds, and credit opportunities.

This second prospect shocked most of the senior bank managers at Access. They had spent much of their professional careers aspiring to the comfort of the corner office. Like captains of navy destroyers, they enjoyed the all-encompassing power they carried in their branches. But now, these admirals-in-waiting were being taken off the bridge, given a well-equipped runabout, and told to wage frontline warfare for the fleet.

At the heart of the bank's plan to recommission its managers as sales staff was a specially designed training course called "Investing for Bank Customers" (IBC). On the surface, IBC taught branch managers about the new investment products they were about to sell and certified them to sell these products. But more broadly and more strategically, the course also introduced these managers to the new world they were about to enter: a world of entrepreneurs, self-starters, and competition, a world where customer service and client satisfaction were key, a world where, after twenty years at the bank, a manager's guaranteed annual income was about to become commission-based. This was a world that, six months ago, most of these people could not even imagine.

Habits, Routine, Culture, and Identity

The American West remains an exciting and innovative part of the American landscape. Dispersed between its metropolitan cities remain tributes to, reminders of, and at times actual links with the older and storied American West. Several miles from town, beyond the reach and interest of suburbia, pavement, and city water, is a place Rebecca and I would venture when city life became overwhelming. It is unfair to call Penny's a bar, as most of her regulars were families. We regularly shared counter space and the barnwood floors with parents who came in from a distant farm for a Budweiser, the latest gossip, and a greasy hamburger while their kids played with toy trucks, dolls, and coloring books on the floor. Penny's always presented an odd and yet welcoming assortment of society. In addition to the farming families exchanging news, a group of young cowhands could be found playing pool, drinking, and swapping stories. A few huge men from the nearby mines were regular dinner guests.

Outside, in Penny's parking lot, our bug-green Subaru seems lost among the perpetual stand of pickup trucks. However, once we are far enough away to safely ostracize ourselves from this automotive symbol of perpetual academia, we are barely noticed.

Rebecca likes Penny's for the grilled cheese sandwiches (they use real Kraft singles). I like it for the conversation and the atmosphere. Today, we've stopped in after taking our dog for a walk along the railway tracks. I'm discussing the perplexities of dog walking with a guy who works at the nearby silver mine. Rather than walking his dog, he lets it loose and then drives off. The dog simply chases him in the car.

"It got to be that the more I walk him, the better shape he gets, the longer I had to walk him," the man reports. "So one day I just said, enough is enough, and now I drive and he runs."

There is a birthday party going on at one end of Penny's, and eight children, some white, some Native American, are trying to pin a tail on a cardboard donkey suspended from the bar. Rebecca is watching *Wheel of Fortune* with Lori, the cook/waitress/barmaid, and losing. During the commercials, we find out that Lori auditioned for the show in Los Angeles just a few months ago. She spent years preparing, watching every show and guessing each word well before the contestants were able to reveal most of the letters. She made it to the semifinal audition in L.A. before faltering. "The auditions are a lot harder than the show," she says with an accusatory glance towards Vanna and Pat, "but I'm gonna go back in six months, and this time I'm gonna make it."

At the other end of the bar, out towards the pool tables, the cowboys are starting to get rowdy. As a stalky, dusty-haired stereotype in black boots reaches into the cooler for a beer, one of his buddies, a taller, bigger version of the first, tells him to put the beer back.

"That's my beer in there and you're not having any of it," he states, matter-of-factly, between pulls on the pool cue he is using to play a practiced game.

"Aw, come on," begs the first guy, and a verbal sparring match gets started as other members of the group join their leader in ostracizing the thirsty outcast. Having watched too many westerns, I'm waiting for one to yell "Draw" or for a chair to fly through the front window. I glance over at Lori to see if she'll reach under the bar for the shotgun barkeepers hide to limit property damage. But the sparring does not escalate. Instead, another cowhand, this one wearing damaged leather chaps over his faded Wrangler jeans, explains that the thirsty one is cut off until he "does his chores." As the conversation progresses, it seems that the cowboy had left the group's common housing without finishing the vacuuming—and this is not the first time he's left a project in midstream. Last week he didn't put the laundry in the dryer, and he refuses to dry the dishes. So, the boys got together and decided that he'd get no beer until the vacuuming got done. And they were all sticking together.

Penny's is a place where people wear their habits on their sleeves. Weary miners pull in for dinner at exactly the same time every day. Lori watches and practices for Wheel of Fortune at 5:30; Rebecca orders grilled cheese and a Coke. Out here, on the edge of the desert, even the pickups in the parking lot are as habitual as the wind and the dust in the air. Young John Wayne here can't have a beer until he's finished the vacuuming. Perhaps even his resistance is routine and habitual. Glancing up at Pat and Vanna, I read aloud the topic "Where the rich and famous go on vacation." Lori looks up at the newly disclosed letters; "Leach's beaches," she says offhandedly.

Our habits and routines are important because they help us interpret and structure daily life without our having to spend a lot of energy and time thinking about it. When things become habitual, we accept them uncritically and often rely on them as touchstones of our larger daily routines. Our habits and routines have a lot to do with who we are and how we fit within our peer groups and communities. Bourdieu uses the term "habitus" to discuss the unconscious acts people employ that link them with their larger social infrastructures.[10] According to Bourdieu, each society has deeply embedded structures that are unconsciously reproduced through people's habitual activities.

Thus, social rules, norms, or behaviors are not enforced and replicated through active monitoring, punishments, or choices but through people's unconscious habits and the social structures that reinforce these habits. For example, the division of labor within a household becomes unquestioned and accepted as normal after generations of mundane activities reinforce and legitimize daily practices. Soon we come to expect certain things because we are habitually used to seeing them happen a specific way. Things get interesting, though, when an activity does not correspond to our version of what is normal: when two calloused cowhands spar about vacuuming and doing the dishes, when a green Subaru is parked among stands of dusty pickup trucks, when bankers start acting like stockbrokers.

Bourdieu's concept is similar to Anthony Giddens's term "routinization," by which he means "the habitual taken-for-granted character of the vast bulk of activities of day-to-day social life."[11] Giddens argues that the repetitive nature of day-to-day life gives most people a sense of security and stability. Therefore, we are more likely to choose familiar, routine events than experiment with unknown, unfamiliar events. According to Giddens, the routinization of daily life allows people to move through activities largely uncritically and without a great deal of self-reflection. These daily routines evolve into habits, then into certainties, and then into bedrock principles. These principles become self-referential and recreate new rituals and rites of passage that only reinforce their own legitimacy.[12] Underlying this process is the often unacknowledged operation of language and the products of language: specialized discourses and stories. Language is unacknowledged because few people are fully conscious about the words they use and the ways these words intersect and thereby sustain or even build beliefs and values. Thus, our specialized discourses and the stories we hear and tell sustain our habits and routines and thereby build our social cultures.

Giddens argues that the routines of culture give life meaning and provide us with a sense of security and belonging. For example, the human rituals that accompany important life events relate individuals to each other and extend the individual into a greater, more encompassing social, intellectual, and emotional plurality. Thus, the seemingly paradoxical hymns of joy sung at a funeral bracket life against traumatic events by providing those mourning with some sense of meaning while still bringing people together to experience grief, sadness, and loss. Given the important role rituals play in life, it is not hard to see why people will resist change and why change can be so threatening. Changing a culture disrupts more than just habits and routines; it calls into question why we do certain things, and it disrupts those very rituals that make sense of our experiences. Giddens calls this an "existential crisis," meaning we lose touch with our reason for being, our self-identity.[13] However, if people desiring change understand the power of the habitual and the routine, and the ways these rituals work to sustain and protect one's identity, changes can be introduced in ways that address and consider the personal and emotional trauma that change may spark.

This was the case at Access as its strategic planners devised ways to change its bankers into brokers. Such a change needed to involve more than simply selling new products or introducing new banking technology. This change was more substantial; it influenced the very ways these senior professionals thought about their jobs. Because it affected the self-identity of these bankers, the changes would alter the very culture of the bank. Emulating the aggressive entrepreneurship of stockbrokers required a different conceptualization of what it meant to be a banker. It required a change in these bankers' daily habits, routines, and naturalized assumptions they made about their profession. To their credit, rather than simply replace their long-term managers, at this point, strategic planners at Access attempted to re-train, or more accurately, re-socialize, these employees.

On the surface, Access's IBC training course certified banking staff to inform the general public about non-bank investments. These bankers could not yet sell investments, but IBC put them on the first step towards that ultimate goal, enabling any bank employee to refer customers to Access's investment specialists. The IBC course was a product of federal regulations that imposed conditions on banks, like Access, who began selling investment products. These regulations were designed to protect members of the general public who, it was generally believed, were likely to confuse investment products with federally insured bank products and who were more likely to trust their neighborhood banker for investment advice before they turned to a stockbroker. At IBC, bankers were taught about the various types of alternative investments and what they had to tell customers when discussing these investments. At the conclusion of the course, the bankers took an exam that officially certified them to refer customers to Access Investments. Federal regulations required that all bank employees who would be referring customers to Access Investments had to take the IBC course and pass the final exam.

If you are in a major city and looking for something to do, walk into any bank, repeat the five magic words "I am interested in investments" to anyone with a name tag, and stand back and watch. If bank officials have done their homework, the banker on the other end of the handshake will try to convince you to meet the bank's investment agent. Then the investment agent will try to persuade you to hand over your money while explaining that none of this money, once handed over, will be insured by the Federal Deposit Insurance Corporation (FDIC). A confusing process. Traditionally, if a bank loses money customers have put in a savings account, the customers will eventually get their money back, provided the deposits are insured by the FDIC. However, if the mutual fund a customer ends up purchasing from the bank's investment specialist goes broke, the customer will lose not only the interest made but also the principal, the amount the customer originally invested. This makes bankers nervous, and most of them have a tough time selling uninsured financial products. That's why they are bankers.

Each banker must fulfill the following federally mandated procedures before they can refer a client to an investment specialist (or sell investments themselves):

1. The banker must conduct a profile of the client's investment experience, willingness, and knowledge before making a sales pitch.
2. The client must be given a full description of all sales charges associated with investments.
3. The client must be given a description of the risks associated with investments, including the potential loss of the principal investment.
4. The client must be told that non-bank investments are not insured by the Federal Deposit Insurance Corporation.

This makes for an awfully tough sales pitch, and despite these very clear requirements, in January 1996, the *Wall Street Journal* reported that many banks were failing to disclose these risks when dealing with customers.[14] Charles Gasparino, a reporter for the *Wall Street Journal,* showed that in a mystery shopping survey conducted by Prophet Market Research and Consulting of San Francisco, "Twenty-seven percent of brokers working at bank branches didn't even tell investors that mutual funds lack federal deposit insurance." In addition, 23 percent of the banks shopped did not profile customers, 23 percent did not describe the sales charges associated with investments, and 11 percent did not discuss the risks associated with these investments.[15] Obviously, it is much easier to hold up the 25 percent rate of return earned by a mutual fund against the 2 percent rate earned by a traditional savings account and then let the customer do the math. However, the sales pitch is often obscured when it comes after the customer profile, the explanation of risk, the small detail about loss of principal, and the final statement about FDIC insurance.

Gasparino's report also recalled various industry studies that indicated that many consumers who purchase mutual funds from banks "believe these investments are somehow safer than those obtained through a brokerage firm," even though they may be purchasing the same product.[16] Such perceptions have certainly helped the banks' efforts to expand into alternative investments. However, this lack of compliance with federal regulations has also led to lawsuits regarding the sale of mutual funds by a Florida bank and, in some extreme cases, to regulators revoking individual and institutional investment licenses. Thus, IBC occurs in a difficult and complex training environment. The course must meet and teach federal compliance requirements while teaching bankers how to compete with the fast-paced, highly competitive, and extremely lucrative world of investment management and securities trading.

Access tried to accomplish this dual goal in two ways. First, IBC placed the changes happening at Access within a historic context, suggesting that the new does not replace the old. Instead, the course argued that changes are required to restore the company's original intentions and achievements. Second, the course attempted to change the language the bankers used in their everyday activities. In this way, IBC tried to get at these professionals' most frequent habits, routines, and ultimately their deeply ingrained business culture.

The new changes at Access represented a significantly reduced role for bank representatives. The branch managers I interviewed and studied were used to being the senior bank representative within their branches, responsible for branch operations and for acting as a gatekeeper who ultimately decides most customers' financial fates. These managers were rewarded for bringing deposits into the branch and for keeping these accounts within the profitable confines of their own branch. The new changes at Access worked to destroy most of what these managers had built over their long careers. Rather than acting as an authority figure, the managers were becoming a liaison between customers and representatives of Access Investments. Managers were no longer responsible for providing financial products; instead, they were required to solicit new business with customers and then deliver these customers to investment dealers throughout Access. Branch representatives who had built their careers by sustaining branch deposit accounts had to now actively work to transfer their best customers' deposits outside their branches to the new investment dealers.

Access justified the reconfiguration of its branch managers' positions by claiming that change was necessary if Access was going to be able to fulfill its historic mission to its customers. In an odd temporal twist, Access argued that its present business had little connection to the bank's historical mission. Thus, in order to be able to fulfill its historical objectives in the future, changes must be made in the present. The claim is oddly backward-looking and yet seductively effective. As the logic goes, banks have always been in the business of helping customers solve their financial problems. However, when their best clients are taking their money to more aggressive investment brokerages to buy home mortgages, finance education, or save for retirement or a large purchase, banks are no longer able to fulfill their traditional, historical, habitual roles.

So, the bank's management argues, in order to keep up their historic mission of "helping customers solve problems," Access must offer the products customers want. At the same time, though branch representatives have historically been able to meet each customer's financial needs, they alone cannot fulfill these needs now that customers are demanding mutual funds, bonds, and other types of specialized investment products. Thus, the branch representative must work in cooperation with specialists in other divisions of the bank to ensure that customers may once again have all of their financial problems solved by the bank. If managers decide to resist change and hold onto their positions of power, they are undermining the historic mission of the bank. If managers agree to radically change their own professional habits and assumptions, they support the bank's new agenda and change along with the bank.

The argument's strength and its controversy lie in the fact that it is based on a presupposition, an assumption embedded within a proposition. In Access's case, the argument for change assumed that this particular crop of managers single-handedly derailed the company from its historic mission. This was an effective assumption because it turned its audience into a scapegoat and forced that audience to actively demonstrate how the argument was incorrect. To resist the argument was only to further ostracize yourself from your employer. To claim the argument was unfair was to step outside a paradigm that had already cast you as an outsider.

Once the bankers conceded their professional autonomy to the new future historical mission of the bank, the IBC course turned its attention to teaching managers how to disrupt their current habits and take on the new position as relationship broker. To accomplish this, the IBC course overtly borrowed instructional strategies and structures from second language learning pedagogies. The IBC course materials overtly made this connection when they noted that one of the goals of the course was "product mastery," which was defined as "being able to think, or talk, or perform with a desired level of correctness and without hesitation." The course materials drew this connection even closer by arguing that learning how to operate in this new banking culture was similar to learning how to be fluent in a foreign language. The course noted that when people have mastered a foreign language, they can speak without thinking or hesitation, they use the right words and grammar, and they can convince their audience that they have known the language for years. Thus, once managers mastered their new role within the bank, they would become fluent within the new culture. They would be able to introduce investments to their customers, answer general questions with certainty and confidence, and feel confident when referring customers to the investment specialists.

Like language acquisition courses, IBC focused on using the new language by writing, speaking, and reading. The course required participants to write answers to question prompts, act out customer relations situations, and present important material to the rest of the class. In addition, the actual product knowledge was learned through repeated oral exercises using cue cards individually and with partners. These cue cards were simple question-and-answer cards with a question on one side and the answer on the other. They asked participants to define things like mutual funds, bonds, investment management services, and a host of other investment related concepts. As the trainer explained to me, the course worked very hard to get participants to use the language of investments in order to make sure that participants not only understood what an IRA was, for example, but also were able to freely use the term in conversation and to make it a regular part of their work day.

Throughout the course, the trainer stressed interpersonal communication skills, often placing participants in customer representative roles and then dictating to them what to say. The trainer would make participants repeat her words, then repeat them to the customer, then repeat them again in conversation. In other cases, the trainer would create a fictional situation and then instruct participants to use the language from their flash cards to solve the problem. Participants' language was tightly restricted as they were allowed only to repeat the phrases on their flash cards or the sentences provided by the trainer. As the class progressed, participants were gradually given more freedom, but only after the language of investments had already penetrated their discourse. Through this direct manipulation of the actual words participants spoke, the course disrupted the bank managers' habitual speech acts, the words they regularly used to conduct daily business. By disrupting these habits and introducing new ones, the bank hoped to change the everyday business culture within the bank.

Identity, Stories, and Change

It has been a particularly unsettling week, and we are heading out to Penny's to unwind and forget about city life for a while. On our way, we stop at the Donner-Reed Museum, located in an old one-room schoolhouse in the last town before the desert and the Sierra Nevada, where most of the ill-fated party of approximately 91 pioneers on their way to California in 1846 met their demise in one of the worst winters ever to bury the mountains. For many westerners, the Donner-Reed story is archetypal of western settlement and what became of pioneers' dreams.

The museum is opened by appointment only, so we get a phone number from a local ice cream and burger hut. About fifteen minutes later Edna Smith, a slight, elderly woman, drives up in a silver Oldsmobile. She greets us and then single-handedly unlocks and opens the immense iron gate blocking the walkway. She then unlocks the padlock at the door and lets us in. Relics the party abandoned on their way across the Salt Lake desert that were later scavenged by others are displayed in glass boxes throughout the room: parts of wagons, oxen yokes, dishes, tools, musical instruments. Though the sampling of the Donner-Reed's artifacts are fascinating, what is more intriguing are the recent additions to the museum. In small piles throughout the room are bricks from the earliest houses in the village. Our guide tells us that she is starting to collect pieces of friends' houses for the museum. She started the collection when she noticed that many of her friends' houses were being torn down after they died. She notes that with "progress," no one has remembered to collect and memorialize the few artifacts or memories that speak about the town's past. On our way out of town, we stop by the local cemetery. One of the markers along the symmetrical rows catches my eye. "Edna Smith," it reads, with a date of birth and a hyphen.

From the Donner-Reed exhibit, we take a back road out to Penny's. The acres of grass, sand, and sky surrounding us remind me of our trip to Topaz, the Japanese internment camp set up in midstate during World War II. Topaz is located along of stretch of land where the clouds seem closer than the nearest town or outpost. After traveling over dirt road after dirt road, we had finally reached the small brown arrow at the side of the road with the words "Topaz" painted in white lettering. We had turned left at the indicated place, crossed through a broken-down fence, and entered Topaz. The site is haunting because there is nothing there. Other than a commemorating plaque and a large interpretive sign riddled with shotgun shells, the 640-acre site that once held 9,408 people is empty. Japanese Americans were forcibly moved into Topaz in September 1942, and the site operated until October 1945. Today, there are only roads and square patches of grass where buildings once stood. We had driven around the site, slowly, looking out for the rabbits and prairie dogs that now make their homes there. The gravel streets made perfectly square corners around remnants of what could have once been the site of a building, a school, a barber shop, a church, a home. Topaz had a compellingly different sense than the Donner-Reed Museum. Encountering Topaz was a little like stumbling onto the Donner-Reed campsite a week after everyone finally got out. Despite the fact that there were no longer any buildings there, a sense remained that nothing had really changed at Topaz since the first tar paper barrack held back the billowing, omnipresent dust and sand. The present confronts the past there in a vigilant, changeless spectacle.

After lunch at Penny's (a habitual grilled cheese sandwich and Coke for Rebecca), we continue on our trip through the West's hazy relationships between past and present. Next on our journey are Ophir and Mercur, two mining towns that date from the mid-1800s. According to local lore, around 1865, soldiers of the United States Army discovered that Indians in the area were using silver bullets. The soldiers found the silver mine and quickly dispatched the Indians. The location was originally named St. Louis but was renamed Ophir in 1870 as a tribute to King Solomon's great mines.[17] The town is now considered a ghost town, as most of its buildings are deserted or uninhabitable. Small cabins, outhouses, and business fronts line the main street, and remnants of rusty mining equipment lie forgotten under rubble, grass, and dirt. However, the town has lately become a bit of a retirement community with local residents taking advantage of the cheap real estate to build dream homes and cottages. There is a village store that doubles as a photo gallery of the old town. On the back wall of the store, black and white photos capture life in Ophir the boom town. Here, groups of men take a brief moment from their mines, stores, bottles, and jail cells to stare at me, Rebecca, and the two other visitors who have momentarily transformed this once prosperous mining town into a tourist attraction.

We buy some soda pop for us and a stick of beef jerky for the dog and travel down and across the canyon to Mercur. A few miles from the town line, we stop to visit the cemetery. Parking at the side of the road, we walk up an embankment and through a collection of shrubs and trees that open to a scattering of neglected crosses, stone graves, and fenced-in plots. If the crosses ever had names on them, a century of wind, snow, sand, and dust long ago erased these historical texts. Back in the car, we find out that the mining company that currently owns Mercur has closed the town to visitors.

According to its web site, Mercur's spirit was resilient. The town was originally named Lewiston and in 1860 was home to a few rugged prospectors. After several successful results, a silver boom took the town by storm until 1880, when the mine ran dry and the city with it. In the mid-1880s, a few prospectors found gold in Mercur's hills, but it proved to be too expensive to extract it from the rock. However, with the backing of several larger investors, the town soon boomed again under the expectations of a new gold rush. Nearly the entire town was burned in 1896 and then again in 1902, but the gold rush boom lasted until 1913. Shortly after, the town was again deserted.

Mercur's spirit was not to be denied, and in 1934 a nearby canyon was found to be rich in gold. By 1936, Mercur was back to its old glory. The glory faded in 1951, when the cost of extraction again made mining operations too expensive. Being nostalgic about these things, I naively hoped that the current mining operations at Mercur might once again revitalize this feisty town. However, late-twentieth-century mining techniques are significantly different than those of 100 years ago, and the town's web site reports that after over 140 years of mining, "Mercur has been strip mined into oblivion."[18]

Now, Mercur exists only symbolically, in the stories people tell; in the crosses, boards, and stones scattered throughout the cemetery; in the images displayed on its web site and in the photographs available at the visitors' center fifty miles from here; and in the lives of the people Rebecca and I meet up with to play *Wheel of Fortune* at Penny's. These people represent the new West, built on the ruins of the old and yet still incorporating the ever-present stories of the old: Edna Smith's quest to memorialize a life lived in a dumping ground for a group of ill-fated western pioneers; a group of senior citizens creating a retirement community among the ghosts of Ophir; cowhands debating house chores over cheeseburgers and Budweiser; an erased town's newest crew of miners and their families; a group of middle-aged bankers learning how to be entrepreneurial customer relations specialists. All of these groups represent a temporal process whereby stories of change reinterpret the past in order to structure a divergent future.

This is why Topaz is so different and so distinct. At the time of our visit to Topaz, very little had been done to interpret, explain, or describe what had happened in the middle of this desert. There was no attempt to teach, direct, or otherwise mediate our experience at Topaz. There were no stories at Topaz, and Topaz seemed to exist without changing. As a consequence, the many social and cultural issues that created Topaz have also seemed to persist without changing. This may be a cruel indictment of over fifty years of cultural reparations. And yet, shortly after we visited Topaz, a federal government building in Oklahoma City was bombed. In the time between the bombing and the eventual arrest of those responsible, media and public attention focused on immigrants, Arabs, and other minority groups who were immediately considered suspects. Several months later, when the population of Quebec, Canada, voted not to separate from English Canada, a leader of Quebec's separatist community blamed the defeat on the "ethnic" vote—and he was not referring to the French or English populations in Quebec.

Our cultural discourses, meaning the jargon, dialects, intonations, vocabularies, and other linguistic features that we use to create and maintain our communities, are important because they make up and reflect the structures that dominate our routinized, habitual world. Whether we are cowhands, miners, pioneers, bankers, or academics, our habitual discourses structure the ways in which we see the world, they communicate the assumptions we carry around with us, and they designate our communities' insiders and outsiders. Within these structures lie the foundations from which we gain our identities as individuals and as part of a larger group of people. To change these structures is to change who we are, what we believe, and how we view each other.

By teaching its branch managers to use a new professional discourse, the trainers at Access hoped to introduce a new sense of self-reflection about the bank managers' habits, routines, and ritual activities in a way that would not efface the managers' self or professional identities but would introduce new identities, new rituals, and new habits. Against this study of cultural change at Access, this chapter has juxtaposed other divergent stories from the West to demonstrate how various agents, past and present, have used their stories to weave new identities as the fabric of the West continues to change. These various stories are part of the changing mosaic that is the West, and, as Giddens notes, such stories of self-identity give coherence and agency to the finite lives people experience within this constantly changing environment.[19] Through their stories, Edna Smith has been changing how her community memorializes its past; the senior citizens at Ophir have changed a mining town into a retirement community; and Penny's miners have paradoxically obliterated yet resurrected Mercur's ghostly spirit. In all of these cases, the language of change presents itself as simultaneously historical and futuristic as the stories of change mediate this movement through the finite structure of time.

Giddens argues that knowing how to use the routines, rituals, and structures embodied in language is to have agency in the face of change.[20] In other words, human agency is enacted when people take the structures of language and use them to create interpretive stories of change. On the one hand, Giddens's model offers a sophisticated accounting for how people can adapt to change. Certainly, that is what Edna Smith, the employees at Access, and the miners at Penny's were doing. On the other hand, even though Giddens's model stresses agency, I cannot help but wonder what kind of agency this is. This model is largely about adapting to change and interpreting change rather than fully understanding change or being able to dramatically influence change. Similarly, Bourdieu's concepts better describe how society reproduces itself and how social elites maintain their positions than how change occurs or why change happens. Therefore, while these theorists offer useful ways of examining the ways people adapt to and resist change, their work still requires an elaborated theory of change.

Critiques of Giddens and Bourdieu appear later in this book (see chapters 5 and 6). For now, I would like to raise one more related story that must be considered before leaving Access and the American West for other stories of change. This is the story of power and of who benefits and who loses from Access's story of change, from Giddens's model of agency, and from my own reporting of this story as a stand-alone observer. In their book *The New Work Order,* James Gee, Glynda Hull, and Colin Lankshear critique "the new capitalism," which they argue has fueled many of the change-management ventures similar to the one I studied at Access.[21] Gee, Hull, and Lankshear cite from a variety of what they call "fast capitalist texts" to piece together a picture and ultimately a social critique of this new capitalist economy.[22] Citing work by Manuel Castells, Gee, Hull, and Lankshear summarize the assumptions of the new capitalism in four ways: (1) productivity is based on knowledge, science, and technology; (2) information and knowledge processing are dominant, key activities for multinational businesses; (3) companies are organized in radically different ways emphasizing flatter organizations, fewer levels of hierarchy, more cooperation, and flexible employees; and (4) competition and the market are now global and focused solely on rapidly fulfilling each individual customer's needs.[23] The changes I witnessed at Access Bank reflect each of these propositions of the new capitalism in the following ways:

1. The bank had placed its full faith in technology in the form of automated teller machines, sophisticated information storage and retrieval software, and even portable telephones in order to reduce its reliance on full-time staff, to target, gain, and manage customers, and to increase the efficiency and decrease the costs of their operations.
2. The changes positioned bank managers as relationship brokers who were responsible for exchanging information between clients and the Access Investment representatives.
3. The levels of hierarchy within the bank were limited to the point that branch managers had little authority or decision-making abilities within their own branches. Each Access employee took on a much larger and more complex decision-making role within the branch.
4. The entire rationale for the bank's changes was to enable it to compete with non-banks (and other bank competitors) to build customer satisfaction and bring clients back to the bank from these other organizations.

Working from two case studies—a team-training course at a factory and a failed manufacturing and sales cooperative in Nicaragua (which had unknowingly adopted much of the new capitalist organizational stance)—Gee, Hull, and Lankshear are critical of the social work accomplished by the new capitalism. Like the argument posed by Access executives, which stated that bank managers were responsible for the bank's departure from its core values yet responsible to bring Access back to those values, Gee, Hull, and Lankshear argue that the rhetoric of the new capitalism is "insulting to workers" despite its desire for fully informed and participatory employees.[24] Although change projects like those implemented by Access talk about empowered workers, information sharing, critical (outside-of-the-box) thinking, and creative expression, employees cannot actually engage in such behavior if the consequences are to the detriment of the organization. The employees only have agency insofar as this agency acts in the interests of the company. Gee, Hull, and Lankshear's argument is worth citing in full:

> The paradox is deeper yet: the newly empowered and newly "critical thinking" workers cannot really question the goals, visions, and values that define the very parameters of the new capitalist business in the new global work order. Such questioning might well mean exiting the new capitalist world and seeking employment in Third World–like, low-wage, marginal jobs in the remaining backwaters of the old capitalism, or having no employment at all. The worker's "freedom" is fixed within the margins of the goals, ends, and vision set by the new capitalism and its theoreticians. The problem can be put another way: real commitment and belief, as well as real learning, require that learners be able to engage in genuine dialogue and contestation with viewpoints, but such genuine contestation is ultimately problematic in a business setting where, in the end, profit is the goal and the competition is at one's heels.[25]

As was the case at Access, if bank managers wanted to argue that the bank's decline was actually because of complacent upper management, a lack of clear leadership, or a bad marriage with Esquire Bank, their dialogue and critical thinking would be considered at best distracting and at worst insubordinate. In fact, during the training sessions, several branch managers did raise complaints and concerns about the merger, the ways the bank was organizing its alternative investment operations, and other bank policies. Each time these issues emerged, however, the trainer stopped the class and wrote the issues down on a "parking lot," which she used to keep track of what she called important but tangential issues.

When Gee, Hull, and Lankshear cite the failure of the Nicaraguan cooperative, they argue that larger global forces associated with the new (and old) capitalism were responsible for the cooperative's demise and not a bad business plan or outdated management theory. The authors argue that factors such as "global and nation-state politics," "historical exploitation," "access to information and education," "the complex workings of technology," and the "winner-take-all nature of contemporary capitalism" are too dominant to be assuaged by new capitalist visions or utopian business models. Thus, from their perspective, the new capitalist vision is nothing more than old wine simply poured into new bottles. Despite the claims of employee agency and accountability, the same dominant structures continue to rule the global playing field.[26]

What is at stake in the new capitalist economy? Gee, Hull, and Lankshear state that the new capitalist argument is about defining a dominant set of cultural values, in the way that churches, governments, and universities have in the past framed values, norms, and belief systems (or in the language of this chapter, habits, routines, and behaviors).[27] The authors argue that this capitalization of our social values must be resisted by developing a new language, what they call a new discourse, that would be opposed to the discourse of the new capitalism. This discourse would privilege the local over the global, emphasize critique as necessary to real learning, and create connections and links among the vast majority of the world's population who have been sidelined by the new capitalist project.[28]

Ultimately, and despite their intentions, Gee, Hull, and Lankshear's proposals seem as utopian as the fast capitalist texts of which they are critical. Perhaps this is part of the authors' intent, to begin to re-create a new oppositional discourse beside the utopian discourses of the new capitalism. However, I would like to position an alternative response to the problematics Gee, Hull, and Lankshear raise and the problematics I found myself facing in my own research at Access. As I mentioned in chapter 2, although my time at Access taught me much about change and about the ways this bank was teaching change, I left the study feeling strangely distanced and unconnected with my subject and my topic. A year after my study had formally completed, I had lunch with one of my informants, who told me that in the end, the bank had embarked on a significant downsizing project and that she was so disillusioned with the way management had so brutally handled this project that she was starting to look around for different employment. As she listed off the managers who were forcibly retired or who had been laid off, I realized that although I had a decent theoretical knowledge of change, I knew very little about the reality of change: the ways these people were living with the implications, threats, insecurities, and unknowns of change. From my protected stance of an observer, I could not fully experience what change really meant to these people. To pretend that I did would be insulting. At the same time, I felt that my accounting of change at Access overemphasized the role of agency. Yes, the model of change I witnessed there did provide agency for employees, but as noted above, this was agency limited within a very narrow scope. There was more going on here, and I did not think that my current position as a researcher would enable me to gain access to the other sides of change.

I left Access looking for a more radical response, a response that required its own discourse and its own radical critique. I saw myself questioning the academic, objectivist researcher position articulated and embodied by work like *The New Work Order.* Inasmuch as Gee, Hull, and Lankshear offer an important and vital discussion of the new capitalism, their reportage perpetuates a tradition of qualitative research that presents three prominent academics who sit apart from their subjects, calmly taking field notes, while those struggling with the actual issues at hand are left to fend for themselves. In fact, in the textual context of interpreting the failures of the Nicaraguan cooperative, Gee, Hull, and Lankshear write, "In September 1995 a Dutch development worker living in a neighboring community reported that a sign on the main highway at the entrance to a lane leading to the cooperative announced that the factory and its machinery were up for sale."[29] In some ways, I see two significant failures here: not only did the cooperative factory fail, but when it did, not one of the researchers who gained so much from having access to this cooperative and its people were present.

I began to suspect that in my juxtapositions of change, storytelling, and academic discourse lay more profound and significant habits, routines, and habitual practices that have as much to do with changing higher education and the function of universities as they do with brokers, bankers, and stories of the wild West. What did the subjects in Gee, Hull, and Lankshear's Third World cooperative gain from their contact with First World researchers? Very few of the workers who were part of the study even had the ability to read the book that was based on their failures. In the same way, what did the people at Access who took valuable time away from their jobs and families to help me gain from my work? What did I do to help them through the bank's changes? What kind of resource was I when my subjects no longer had the jobs I continued to describe in conference papers and journal articles?

Is it any wonder why many of these people are now antagonistic towards academics, universities, and higher education? In the nearly two decades of dramatic and sweeping changes in corporate America, changes that included massive layoffs, technological revolutions, increased educational needs, and organizational restructuring, academic researchers largely have remained on the sidelines, commenting and critiquing but rarely acting. This is readily seen in the fact that business trade books (the "fast capitalist texts" that Gee, Hull, and Lankshear cite) are widely read and followed in business contexts while academic publications are rarely acknowledged.

Gee, Hull, and Lankshear are right when they argue that those opposing the new capitalism need a new discourse, just as those looking to preserve the integrity and vitality of the university need a new discourse. However, what we and what they have yet to realize is that this new discourse must start with a self-reflexive analysis of our own languages and stories of research before it can usefully appear in someone else's language of education. The chapters that follow are an attempt to help build this new discourse.

4 ▪ NARRATIVES AND ORGANIZATIONAL
CHANGE: STORIES FROM ACADEME

Higher Education and Change

November 1997, Thanksgiving weekend. We are flying to the coast to meet Tim, a friend from my undergraduate days at the University of Waterloo. After a brief tour of the atmospheric sciences department, where Tim is doing his graduate work, we will be renting a car and driving into the mountains to spend Thanksgiving weekend with Tim's girlfriend and her family. We've only met Traci once, but she was enthusiastic about our crashing her family's annual event. We pick Tim up at the university and head out to the mountains.

So far, the weekend has gone exceptionally well. Our rental car has been upgraded to a full-size Toyota Camry with electronic traction control. We left the rain behind in the city, and I'm enjoying throwing the Camry's willing six cylinders into the road's winding corners. As we gain in elevation, my test drive is slowed by a light dusting of snow on the road. Half an hour later, the snow is building on the road and on the Camry's window wipers. We arrive at Traci's home in time to watch the light pellets turn into large, dense flakes. The family home is seated at the far end of an oval-shaped valley, tucked into the foothills of the nearby mountains and surrounded on three sides by tall, spiraling pines. The location is spectacular. Our approach is guided by a field that stretches out in front of the house. Traci's Volvo is parked in front of a three-car garage built into the hill underneath the house. Atop the garage, a railed deck stretches towards a screened porch and a brightly lit kitchen. Sunlight radiates through the snow, reflecting off the windows that cover the greater part of the building's exterior. I'm so impressed by our weekend resort that I don't even notice the first snowball smash into the Camry's front window. The second smash startles me, and we are soon embroiled in a full-scale snowball-driven assault on the house. Once we breach the house, Traci greets us and runs towards an already warm VW bus. We hurry to catch up to her mom and dad, who are just about to go skiing. The four of us pile into the bus.

Our adventure is enjoyable, punctuated with brilliant vistas and breathtaking views of the mountains. The trail is actually a mountain road that the highway department closes after September. Peter explained that too many people got stuck or slid off in the winter, so they decided it was simpler to just close the thing after the summer.

We climb out of the van, sort through a collection of skis, boots, and poles, and begin our ascent. Peter and Lydia have done this far more often than we have, and after ten minutes we can no longer see them. Traci is caught in the middle, wanting to stretch her legs but feeling some obligation towards her rookie visitors.

Shortly, she is gone, too. Tim, Rebecca, and I soldier on. I briefly recall that only this morning I was getting on an airplane, and just a few hours ago I was enjoying a raspberry mocha downtown. Suddenly feeling disoriented, I wipe out.

The rest of our trek is relatively uneventful. Peter, Lydia, and Traci eventually emerge from the clouds ahead to pass us on their way back down the trail. We see that as a good enough reason to turn around and head back to the VW.

Back at the base camp, Traci helps us unpack, and Tim helps himself to the hot chocolate. The stone mugs warm our hands as Traci takes us on the tour. The home's interior is post and beam with windows that seem to reach out and embrace pine trees, meadows, and mountain peaks at every turn. Tim joins us as we head downstairs.

"This is Peter's office," Tim explains as we head down a dimly lit staircase. The bottom of the stairwell is brightly lit by the still unseen windows that must light the room. The last step reveals what must be a thirty-square-foot room ringed by computers, monitors, electronic monitoring devices, some kind of huge radio receivers, and other assorted electronic equipment. Their red and green lights are flashing in an asynchronous rhythm. On the far wall, a giant printer is mapping out frequencies on a rolling chart of paper, its long arm etching a jagged line down the middle of a three-foot page. The setup is far more comprehensive than anything I've seen before.

Looking at Tim, I'm lost for words. "Should we be here?" Rebecca asks. "I mean, is this something we should know about?"

"Oh, sure," Tim takes over. Oddly, he is much more comfortable in this technological wonderment than Traci our tour guide. "Cool stuff, isn't it? Most universities would die for a lab like this." Tim explains that Peter is a research scientist who studies ice cap melting, water currents, and other atmospheric phenomena. He was tenured at a state university, but his major research sponsors were becoming frustrated because over half of the grant money they gave to Peter for research was taken as overhead by the university. One day his sponsors approached Peter and offered to set him up in his own laboratory away from the university if he could guarantee that their grant money would go only to his salary and research. Peter resigned his full-time position and built this dream house and lab on his wife's family property. He still maintains a fledgling connection with his old university, but he no longer teaches classes, mentors graduate students, or deals with university administration. His priorities are his research, his skiing, and his brother-in-law's apple orchard. Every so often he travels out to an ice cap or a remote ocean site to deposit various monitors that transmit signals to his lab via satellite. We climb back up the stairs, and Tim locks the door. "Lydia's family is coming over for dinner tomorrow, so it's best if we keep the lab locked."

Over dinner, Peter explains that in the end, he sees this move as an ethical decision. He argues that his research clients were paying considerable money for his research, but the university was taking nearly half their investment in overhead. So, for less money, his funding agency gets him full time, and he works exclusively for them. Peter continues to publish his data when relevant and keeps up with conferences, journals, and larger debates in the field. He argues that for him, it is more freeing to be able to work on his own without all the trappings of a university system. He can hire whomever he wants for research assistance, guaranteeing him qualified help; he does not teach; he has no grading, no mediocre students who are more interested in grades than learning, no committee work; his equipment is always up-to-date; and he is not always looking for research money. He presents this list as if he has presented it many, many times before. He probably has.

We rarely think about an educational institution as an organization, a workplace, or even a business. Yet, like any other organization, schools have stories. These stories encapsulate the school's mission, the relationships it hopes to build among students, teachers, parents, and the community. However, like any other organization, schools can become distressed and dysfunctional. They can generate negative images, alienate students, isolate teachers, and upset their communities. Though many educators shudder when schools are discussed using the same concepts and images as a business, we often overlook the ways that organizational dynamics occur in schools and the implications that these dynamics have on a school's educational mission.

Peter's comments were a stinging and perhaps extreme indictment of universities and the system of higher education in America. Yet, for many stakeholders, these issues are very real. They were very real for Peter, who chose to sidestep the entire university system in order to conduct his research in ways he found to be more cost-effective and ultimately more valuable for himself and his clients. For Peter, the university system was too constraining and could not offer him the kind of quality he needed. He found teaching, grading, and student consultations too time consuming and only minimally productive. His clients were equally critical about the university system, choosing to abandon any connection their research needs might spark between teaching and research and instead deciding to subcontract out to a lone researcher in rural Washington State.

Credibility in education also became very real for me in my first year living in a midsized city in the Canadian West. As I mentioned earlier, when I decided to adopt the position of an academic consultant, my goal was to work with nonprofit organizations and to specialize in the area of change-management. My larger goal was to build some necessary links between my academic training and the community in which I was living. One of my first clients was the massage therapy program at MacKenzie College. MacKenzie College was no giant land grant university, nor was it an exclusive, elite Ivy League school. It was a small, technical, career-oriented school that desperately needed some help understanding and repairing a deteriorating educational climate. Given my interest in education, schools, and change, this seemed like a natural place to start my practice.

MacKenzie College

MacKenzie College offers one- and two-year programs in a variety of career skills, including travel and tourism, computer repair, security, and massage therapy. The massage therapy program teaches principles and theories of massage (often called "bodywork"), training students for careers with sports teams, alternative health care providers, tourist venues (cruise ships, resorts), and private practices. It is a two-year program, consisting of course work, practical instruction, and service in MacKenzie's public "drop-in" massage therapy clinic. Students must complete all of their required courses, a minimum number of practical hours, and a minimum number of service hours in the drop-in clinic before they can graduate as registered massage therapists.

MacKenzie's program in massage therapy is part of a growing alternative health care industry. In addition to an increasing number of private massage therapy practitioners, several large American corporations, including Intuit, Cigna, and StorageTek, offer on-site massage therapy programs for employees. In October 1998, Blue Cross and Blue Shield of Georgia and United HealthCare of Colorado began offering partial coverage of massage therapy as an alternative medical practice.

Despite this recent growth of successful, legitimate, and lucrative massage therapy practices, MacKenzie's massage therapy program had developed a deteriorating organizational culture. The school was having problems retaining students and was unable to turn the recent growth and successes of massage therapy as a field into an asset at the school. Students were antagonistic towards instructors and administrators; instructors argued that the students were ill-prepared and unmotivated; administrators had issues with both groups.

The problems experienced at MacKenzie were not the expansive, national, systematic problems cited by people like Lewis and Smith or Thomas Moore. Instead, its problems concerned the everyday, practical running of a specialized school. But, at the same time, some of these larger issues were apparent in the troubles MacKenzie was facing, and in our ultimate solutions, we applied strategies that could have direct application to some of these larger issues.

Throughout my time at MacKenzie College, I worked with a bright, entrepreneurial, and dedicated registered massage therapist named Neil. Neil had only recently been appointed director of MacKenzie's massage therapy program, and his explicit task as director was to fix the massage school's many problems and successfully change its organizational culture. When I first spoke with Neil, he summed up the atmosphere at MacKenzie by saying that the school was developing a significant "us versus them" culture: All of the school's major issues seemed to come down to the opposition between the students and the instructors and administrators. Discipline problems were increasing, more and more students were late for classes or were missing classes, and students were regularly failing exams and not completing homework. Neil said he seemed to be always waiting for the next big issue to boil over.

Neil suspected that a large part of the school's problem stemmed from his administration's inability to communicate its goals and objectives with MacKenzie's students, and he believed that much of this difficulty resulted from his predecessor's "casual" approach to MacKenzie's professional culture. MacKenzie had never had a sexual harassment policy, a consistent examinations policy, an official appeals process, or an official code of conduct for students and instructors. My task, Neil suggested, was to examine and evaluate MacKenzie's current communications, determine its weaknesses and problems, and put in place a long-term solution that would benefit MacKenzie's students, instructors, and administrators. The project seemed interesting, if a little odd, and challenging.

The Operations of Structure

Before I made my first official visit to MacKenzie College, I spent some time reviewing what other people have written about student behavior. In his book *Learning to Labor,* educationalist Paul Willis details a study of negative student behavior he completed in northern England.[1] Willis studied the behaviors, activities, successes, and failures of twelve nonacademic, working-class boys. Rather than simply discount these students' behavior as deviant or immature, Willis eventually argued that the activities in which these students engaged were group-building activities that solidified lower-class students against the school's dominant middle-class culture. For these boys, the "good behavior" expected by the school meant conforming to an unknown culture that required them to betray their personal, familial, and social identity. Working-class students had their own stories about the world, the school, and success, and they didn't believe the stories told by their middle-class colleagues. To make matters worse, the school system was not interested in the boys' stories or their unique cultural experiences.

Willis's findings are shared by American educationalist Henry Giroux.[2] Giroux argues that the oppositional behavior seen in schools is often a result of students enacting forms of solidarity and resistance. These behaviors are usually presented through symbolic activities: dress, aesthetic taste, language, and other visible signs of opposition. Through these acts of symbolic resistance, students form groups, express opinions, create social hierarchies, and show their opposition to teachers, administrators, and other forms of power. Giroux cautions that not all acts of oppositional behavior should be seen as resistance. He argues that each individual's behavior must be held up against his or her "lived experience" within the organization. Actual resistant behavior will be linked to struggles against domination or submission and will thereby seek to change forms of power within an organization. Put in the terms introduced in the previous chapter, these educational theorists seem to be pointing to a battle between the structures of education on the one side and students' desire to express their agency as distinct individuals from distinct cultures on the other.

In the previous chapter, I argued that human agency is enacted when people take the structures of language and use them to create interpretive stories of change. While nothing that happened at MacKenzie or at Access Bank has made me doubt this claim, I think that this statement needs to be elaborated a bit more. What do we mean by "the structures of language"? How can we uncover these structures? What is the relationship between structure, agency, and change? By focusing on these questions and further examining the interrelations between structure, agency, and change, we can add to the social theories developed in chapter 3 and begin to build a better theoretical explanation for social and organizational change.

When considering the problems of agency and structure, it is easy to get caught up in agency, the more overtly romantic side of this picture. Agency seems more emancipatory, it seeks alternatives, and it appears more positive and humane. For example, the review of Willis's and Giroux's studies presented above emphasized student agency: students' activities, behaviors, and values and how these behaviors point to the ways students resisted and acted against institutional dominance. Against such studies, structure seems overpoweringly bleak, totalizing, helpless. Fairclough summarizes this position well when he argues that "too great a focus upon structures is tantamount to taking a one-sided perspective in respect to [human] struggles."[3] Fairclough contends that focusing on structure emphasizes the powerful, the preservation of social order, and the forces that dominate and control rather than the forces of resistance and struggle. If structure is about domination, agency seems to be about underdogs. And we like underdogs.

But this is a source of real trouble in social theory. In embracing agency, people forget about structure and underestimate or forget about the power of structure. Worse, in emphasizing agency, we can too easily reproduce or fall into existing repressive structures. Although I claimed in chapter 2 that people at Access Bank and Penny's used language to assert agency, we can question how much agency they really had. To some extent, their storytelling only re-situated them back within their own structures. Perhaps this is what they wanted, to keep pace with change so they would never feel completely out of step with the changes that were happening around them. In this case, they had agency, but their agency was only useful insofar as it adapted to larger economic or social structures. But what if they wanted to create a deeper change? What if they wanted to create a structural change in the world around them? How might such a change be described and how might it be accomplished?

These were some of the questions examined by French philosopher Michel Foucault. Traditionally, structuralism is associated with forms of linguistics (Chomsky), political economy (Marx), and some forms of psychology (psychoanalysis, Lacan). Structural studies are known for seeking primary, universal foundations upon which objective systems operate. For example, structural linguists work from the assumption that a universal grammar, common to all humans, exists, and their own research will work to further uncover and reveal this structure.

Foucault's project was different. He was critical of structuralism and its claims of a uniting theory, and he distanced himself from structuralist projects that tried to map underlying universal principles. Foucault was interested in how structures change. He saw structures as temporal constructions that emerge, for a time, as powerful and influential ways of thinking, acting, and behaving. However, rather than being universally predetermining, he argued that structures compete with and replace each other as they battle for legitimacy and social power. For example, in the conclusion to his book *The Order of Things*, Foucault offers perhaps one of his most famous images, a comment on the longevity of "man" as an intellectual structure: "Man is neither the oldest nor the most constant problem that has been posed for human knowledge. . . . Man is a recent invention. . . . And one perhaps nearing its end. . . . One can certainly wager that man would be erased, like a face drawn in the sand at the edge of the sea."[4] Here, Foucault is not writing about the physical extinction of humanity. Instead, he argues that "man," as an intellectual structure, has not, and probably will not, always be recognized as a unique, overarching, or even useful concept.

In investigating structures, Foucault was interested less in the system itself than what gave rise to the system, what David Macey calls "the 'operations' that gave rise to the said system."[5] Rather than simply mapping and thereby acquiescing to structures, Foucault sought to dismantle structures by showing the conditions, assumptions, and power relations that give structures their credibility and their ability to control. Foucault's interest in unmasking the structures of social systems can be seen throughout his extensive work on modern organizations. His analysis is concerned with how western culture is increasingly dominated by organizations, institutions, and the values engendered by these entities.[6]

Throughout this work, Foucault sees the rise of the modern organization, and its reification as an institution, as a principal threat to individual autonomy and personal agency. For this reason, he argued that modernity's embrace of organizational power must be met with a renewed articulation of individual ethics.[7] But rather than develop a humanist ethics based on what people should do or what they should think, Foucault articulated a more analytical ethic, one that would examine how an organization's structures and practices define and construct the individual. For example, one would investigate how structures of education construct student identity; how structures of medicine define patients and sickness; how psychology defines who is and who is not insane. Foucault was especially interested in cases when organizations and institutions identify and thereby construct an individual against the individual's will or without his or her knowledge. Foucault wanted to introduce a way to investigate how this happens and how structures gain such powerful social, economic, and cultural positions.

Foucault's interest in organizations and institutions was initiated with his doctoral dissertation, a historical examination of the field of psychiatry. Published as *Madness and Civilization*, this analysis traces the technical discourse on madness, showing how the project of psychiatry came to define, evaluate, and ultimately institutionalize mental illness.[8] The book's conclusions demonstrate the ways the pseudoscientific category "madness" became a powerful instrument of social normalization and control. As a technical term, madness was able to explain great moments of creativity, ridicule opposing viewpoints, and justify antisocial behavior. At the same time, the threat of being called mad was used to force people's compliance with existing beliefs and traditions.

Madness and Civilization initiated an important theme that continued throughout Foucault's work. In later examinations of medicine *(The Birth of the Clinic)*, law *(Discipline and Punish)*, and sexuality *(The History of Sexuality)*, Foucault sought to identify naturalized structures that categorize and define people.[9] Thus, psychiatry institutionalized madness, medicine institutionalized sickness, law institutionalized deviant behavior, and the church institutionalized sexual relations. In the process, Foucault writes, individual citizens gave the right to define themselves to a new class of experts, or professionals, who used special knowledge to categorize and define.

After studying the rise of these modern institutions, Foucault began to discuss what he saw as greater similarities than differences among institutions. For Foucault, prisons resembled factories, schools, barracks, and hospitals, which in turn all resembled prisons.[10] This claim was based on his finding that each of these institutions specialized in defining what is normal and then correcting (disciplining) what it saw as abnormal. I will pick up this point again in chapter 5, but for now, it is important to see that Foucault's analysis was not a straightforward indictment of organizations, nor was it a conclusion that humans were forever entrapped by their own structures. Instead, Foucault argued that analysis needs to rigorously investigate structures, wherever they appear, and thereby demonstrate how humans have become unknowingly complicit with organizational power. Such analysis would show how people have taken for granted medical, legal, governmental, or pedagogical authority and voluntarily (or unconsciously) allowed themselves to be defined according to these structures. For Foucault, agency could not occur without a careful delineation of structure, because agency could only happen in specific relation to structure. The ways we act, think, and even become creative are known to us only through the intellectual, emotional, spiritual, and aesthetic structures that frame our world. Thus, to change the ways we behave, think, or learn requires a change in the structures we use to interpret and frame daily life.

However difficult this may seem, this was exactly the kind of change that needed to be made at MacKenzie College.

Reading the Narratives of MacKenzie College

My first official visit to MacKenzie occurred on a brisk autumn morning. It was the time of year when snow hangs in the wind and rivers begin to gel in anticipation of winter. I had chosen to walk from my home to MacKenzie College, thinking that the distance would give me time to mentally prepare for the day's interviews with students, faculty, and administrators. By the time I saw MacKenzie's bright blue and red sign, my numbed hands and swollen fingers were regretting this decision. MacKenzie is located on the outskirts of the city's downtown core, just beyond four city blocks that form a commercial wedge against the slum housing, industrial park, and roadways that constitute the rest of downtown. MacKenzie's marginal geographic position is directly proportionate to its social and academic standing. MacKenzie attracts students who have narrowly completed high school and are now seeking what they call a "more practical" alternative to a four-year college degree. Scattered among these students are adults who would otherwise be officially unemployed. Their tuition is paid through a welfare program that provides monthly stipends and tuition for unemployed adults who enroll in a work training program.

From the outside, MacKenzie looks more like a small office building than a school. Built in the late 1950s, the four-story building is red brick. Black fire escapes cascade off its back into a gravel alley filled with uncollected refuse. A gravel parking lot borders MacKenzie's left side and a series of diners its right. Three doors down, an "alternative" book store and coffee shop complete the streetscape. MacKenzie's front entrance was built as a tunnel leading to two glass doors. Since the college prohibits smoking indoors, the tunnel has become a popular place for students to hang out and smoke between classes. On my way into the school, I passed through a crowd of students who, on first glance, appeared to be bracing the wall from falling into the pool of cigarette butts that carpeted the sidewalk. The tunnel's white ceiling was stained gray. The smoke was thick and overpowering.

My nicotine-charged encounter with MacKenzie's students provided me with the same unfortunate first encounter most people receive when they visit the college. It is an impression faculty and administration have been trying to combat for months. As Neil, the director of MacKenzie's massage therapy program, noted, this is not an atmosphere most people would associate with therapeutic healing and relaxation. However, this concern with the college's external image was only a small indication of the larger problems at the massage program. In my later interviews with instructors and administrators, I was told that students were rude, impatient, and unresponsive to staff's directions and instructions. Instructors noted that students rarely completed their homework, were often obnoxious and antagonistic in class, and seemed to purposely go out of their way to confront authority. For example, since massage therapy is closely aligned with health care and its practitioners strive to develop comfortable, healthy, therapeutic environments, the massage school instructors asked students to dress respectfully both in class and when working at the drop-in clinic. However, the instructors complained that even after repeated reminders of the school's dress policy, students still attended class and clinic in dirty, faded jeans (often with holes in the knees or rear), T-shirts with inappropriate slogans and logos, and baseball hats (usually worn backwards). They would demand that the students remove their hats in class, but the next day the students would come still wearing hats. As one instructor told me, it seemed like such a no-win situation that he finally stopped remarking about the hats. Other instructors complained that students chewed gum while performing massages, and some wore strong perfumes and colognes both in class and in the clinic. "Some days," one instructor noted, "between the aroma oils we use for the massage, the perfume, and the cologne, it's nearly impossible to breathe in here."

Neil's office was a cross between a physician's office and the graduate student enclave found in most universities. Three desks were spaced around the room, a six-person mail tray hung from the wall, and a wobbly coat rack was propped in the corner, beside which a full-scale human skeleton stood. Three posters illustrating the body's muscular infrastructure were grouped along the back wall, and a set of medical encyclopedias clung to a crooked book-shelf. White lab coats were flung onto the coat rack and the skeleton's shoulder. Behind a dark paneled wood door in the far corner of the office was the bathroom, and a colorful chart adorned the wall beside the door. Written in red marker along the top of the chart was the statement, "Our mission is to provide a learning environment which facilitates self-confidence, knowledge and professionalism in the practice of therapeutic massage." Neil welcomed me at the door and followed my eye to the motivational chart. "That was the result of our last consultant," he said. "Pretty much a waste of time."

Neil led me to a small classroom where sixteen students were gathering around eight massage tables. "This is our senior class," Neil remarked. "They will be graduating this winter, and many of them have already had several job offers. Today is their twice-a-week practical senior seminar." Bruce, the course instructor, was already at the front of the class, impatiently waiting to start. Neil offered a quick introduction, causing the class to erupt in wisecracks and laughter when he said that I was here to find a way to solve the communication breakdown between the students and the instructors and administrators. One student half-seriously objected to Neil's project, saying that his class had endured these problems for two years, "so why should the younger classes have it any easier?" Neil smiled and faked a punch in the student's direction as he left me with Bruce.

"Okay," Bruce said, "today we are going to practice the deep touching we discussed last class. Team up and I'll be around to see how you are doing."

Eight of the students started stripping off their clothing. There were no screens, dividers, coat racks, or shelves, so the students simply dropped their T-shirts and jeans on the floor as they climbed the massage tables. Covered only by small white towels, students laid on their fronts or sides as their partners started massaging arms, legs, and backs. Bruce began to circulate around the room, offering criticism and suggestions and asking each student how the treatment felt. Though Bruce and I had agreed that I could ask students questions during the class, I wasn't sure where to look, not to mention what to ask. A woman on the second table having her calf muscle worked on by a male colleague abruptly sat up and asked if I had any questions. Sensing my discomfort, she remarked, "Oh, does this bother you?" referring to the fact that she was naked.

"What did you expect," joked the man working on her lower leg, "bathing suits?" The other students laughed.

"Oh, we're used to it by now," said the woman, reclining to her prior position. "After two years of this, you really get to know each other."

"Maybe a little too well," punctuated a female student who had started massaging a colleague's upper back. Bruce said that if I was uncomfortable, he could look around for gowns for the students.

For the next forty-five minutes, the students practiced various massage techniques on each other while Bruce circulated around the room and I did my best to talk with them about their experience at the school, study habits, exams, job offers, and what they had learned about massage during their two years at MacKenzie. After the first set of students had manipulated, stretched, and, at times, coerced sufficient body parts, they took their turn on the tables while the others switched for revenge. Occasionally, I saw a painful grimace or heard a loud shout followed by a meek "Sorry." Bruce seemed to be a patient instructor. He monitored each student's activities, quietly adjusting hands, fingers, or arms when required, explaining why these adjusted techniques were more effective.

At the conclusion of the class, Bruce left me to interview the students about the various administrative problems they had faced, their perceptions of the school's faculty, and their recommendations for new students just starting off in massage therapy. Once dressed, the students told me about their early days in the program; the difficulty some of the older students had experienced coming back to school after several years of working; the work load, which was much greater than in high school; and the immense time commitment the program required. "It basically becomes your life for two years," noted one woman. The students stated that they were not told about these hours until they were registered in the program and started talking to other students. Additionally, they did not know that the course required a significant number of hours at the drop-in clinic, working on real patients. The students also told me that they were unprepared for the occasional offensive "propositions" they received when working at the clinic. At the conclusion of our interview, the senior class agreed to meet with me again after I had the opportunity to see a bit more of the school.

My next meeting was with a group of first-year, first-term students as I attended their anatomy course. The classroom was upstairs, where Bruce introduced me to Kurt, the class instructor. Kurt did not think much of my project, and he complained that the school's high drop-out rate was largely a result of poor student quality. "They are not good students" he said, "and our standards are simply not high enough. If we would be more selective, we wouldn't lose nearly as many as we do." That said, Kurt led me into his class, where about thirty-five students were seated in rows facing the chalkboard. As their instructors had noted, the students were dressed in faded, ripped jeans and T-shirts. Most of the men were wearing baseball hats, and the women wore sweatshirts. Several students were wearing cotton sweatpants. Kurt started the class by reviewing material for an upcoming midterm exam.

After thirty minutes, Kurt stopped his review. He told the drowsy students to take a brief five-minute break; when they came back, they would do some exercises to understand and gauge "the curvature of the spine." Ten minutes later, the students gravitated towards their desks as Kurt began to review ways to evaluate the contour of a person's spine. According to Kurt's method, the therapist uses a marker to place a small dot on the skin at each of the individual vertebra's bony elevations. Next, the therapist hangs a thin cord or piece of string from the ceiling and has the patient stand with his or her back to the rope. With plumb line in hand, the therapist eyeballs any black dots that do not align properly. Kurt taught that extreme deviations from the plumb should be noted and the patient referred to a medical physician or chiropractor. "Remember," he cautioned, "we don't want to do any damage or make already bad conditions worse. If you suspect a medical problem that massage cannot adequately treat, that person should be referred to a medical doctor."

Kurt then required the class to team up in pairs to map each other's spine. However, unlike the graduating seniors in my first classroom encounter, these students were extremely uncomfortable with Kurt's instructions. They took several minutes to team up and get the necessary markers and string, then took a good ten minutes to hang their plumb lines. Unlike the senior class, these first-term students divided into gender-exclusive teams, men working together and women working together, and after about ten minutes, most of the male teams had set up their plumb lines and were about to start the first analysis. The women were still debating who would go first. Kurt took no notice of the women's discomfort and instead walked among the male groups, examining their progress. Eventually, two older women took the initiative and removed their shirts, and their partners started mapping their spines. Now that the ice had been broken, the other women grudgingly complied with Kurt's instructions. However, the women faced away from the men as their partners worked. The dangling plumb lines mirrored the tension in the class. The groups worked in silence; there was none of the joking and camaraderie that the seniors had shared. Kurt's comment did not help: "Ladies, that's not going to do it," he said, referring to the fact that some women had not fully removed their shirts. "You are not going to be able to offer an accurate evaluation unless you can properly see the full line of the spine." Kurt's challenge was met once again by the two senior women in the class, who jokingly announced that "they had nothing to hide"; however, the majority of women ignored Kurt's chastising and silently finished their work.

Later that afternoon, I met once again with the senior class and told them about the tension I had found in the first-year class. "Oh, they'll get over it; we did," was the consensus of the group. The seniors told me how they had been reticent about numerous issues they had encountered their first year, including the nudity in the classroom, the touching and being touched, and the intense physicality of the course. The students said that it had been extremely difficult and uncomfortable when the class first began practicing massage techniques on each other. However, it had been even more difficult once they started working in the clinic and began massaging strangers. They noted that most of the people who did drop out left during these first six months.

Additionally, students said that it was very hard being the person on whom their colleagues practiced. They noted how sore, bruised, and tired they were after a day of practice, especially when the students performing the massages were learning new techniques. "We all mess up," said one student, "and it's easy to stretch a muscle too far or not know that you're working too hard, and you end up bruising somebody." Students said that there were days when they didn't want to come to class because they knew they would go home sore, and they often felt resentful and angry when someone hurt them.

The students also noted that their families did not understand the pressures and time commitments involved with massage school. Students told me that they would often come home from a day of technique and a family member would want a massage. They indicated that at first, it was tough to say no, but soon they were giving massages to everyone in their family and to their friends, and then they would come to school and do it all over again. According to the students, this cycle created resentment towards family members, colleagues at school, and the school itself. Massage was no longer something soothing and relaxing; instead, it became a duty and oftentimes a painful experience. "It's important to get away from it," a student noted, "so you can heal up and come back with a clear head."

When I asked the students how they coped with their families and friends and with the physical and academic demands of the program, the seniors spoke about establishing personal boundaries, enforcing them, and knowing when they had been violated. They also spoke about changing one's boundaries—some days they were more or less comfortable with their peers. At first, some were uncomfortable telling each other that a technique was painful or that they did not want to give their sister a massage when they came home from school. However, most said that after a particularly stressful time, they learned to say no. This stress was called "a complete breakdown" or "going nuts" or "getting sick" and was identified as a period when students' grades were falling, they were missing school, and they were angry and resentful with their family, friends, and colleagues at school. If the students could survive this "breakdown," they could look forward to graduating from the program.

The Discursive Structures of Change

In his book *The Archaeology of Knowledge,* Foucault outlined what he called an "archaeological description of change."[11] *The Archaeology of Knowledge* is a complex, methodological book concerned with how one should go about researching and interpreting the formation of human knowledge. (Foucault did not take on small projects.) What emerges from this work is an analysis based on the examination of discourse, meaning language-in-use. This analysis examines "statements in the field of discourse and the relations of which they are capable."[12] In other words, the analysis looks at the immediate discourse one encounters in any situation and examines what other discourses, statements, or languages enable this particular discourse to exist. The analysis also investigates how this discourse has become influential at this point in time and in this location and what this discourse could enable in the future.

Such a project does not simply trace the historical derivatives of words but involves seeing language as an active, complex, and strategic system of privilege, responsibility, power, and tradition. According to Foucault, nothing can exist outside of discourse. This is because we can know something only through the discourse used to investigate, assess, and interpret it. As Macey notes, Foucault's method "is not concerned with physical objects, but with the discursive process which makes it possible to speak about objects."[13] Thus, the task of an investigator is to describe the connections between discourse and knowledge and show how this connection ultimately informs beliefs and practices.[14]

It is not surprising, then, that Foucault's *Archaeology* locates moments of change within the specific discourses people use. Foucault would predict that as something changes, the ways people speak and write about it will also change. Similarly, if people reject new discourses, they are also struggling against and resisting change. For Foucault, change occurs as a process of discursive struggle, and archaeology shows "on what condition a correlation can exist" between new statements and change. Archaeology sets up what is possible within "the very density of discourse." Thus, it is not enough to simply suggest that things have changed, or to point to discourses and show that change has occurred. Instead, "we must define precisely what these changes consist of" by establishing what Foucault calls "a system of transformation."[15] This would be a record of how one discourse came to replace or supplant another, followed by an ongoing process that would monitor continuous discursive replacements. Foucault is careful to argue that this process does not often happen all at once. A new discourse does not appear fully formed and complete; instead, it slowly develops and emerges as it pushes out the old discourse and the old system attached to that discourse.

Although Foucault's model is designed as a way to study change and transformation, I saw it as a powerful way to introduce change within MacKenzie College. First, I articulated the various discourses that I believed were creating MacKenzie's current organizational culture. Then, Neil and I introduced new discourses at various places within the school as a way to erode the existing discourses and supplant them with new ones. Thus, our efforts were targeted at MacKenzie's narratives, the tales people within the organization were telling each other. Our task was first to read these narratives; then we could begin to alter them.

Reading Narratives, Writing Change

From my "reading" of MacKenzie, four narratives—or rather, a lack of organizational narratives—emerged. Together, they pointed to several serious problems with MacKenzie's organizational culture. First, MacKenzie did not have important organizational structures in place to protect students, instructors, and clients. Despite the obvious risks for sexual abuse and harassment in MacKenzie's classrooms and clinics, MacKenzie did not have official policies in place to deal with this risk. Additionally, MacKenzie did not have official codes of conduct for students and instructors, nor did it have policies on discrimination or equal opportunities for students. In fact, there was no narrative or language students could use if they felt violated, hurt, or insulted. So, in place of an official narrative from the college, the students invented, repeated, and reinforced their own narrative, which ran something like the report I received from the senior class: *Being part of a massage school means that you're going to face some difficult situations. Be sure to find ways to deal with this, because you're not going to get much help. Mostly, learn to get over it and deal with it.*

Second, the massage school students were not prepared for the time commitment and work load required by MacKenzie's curriculum. Most students had completed only high school and did not have sufficient academic proficiency to attend a university. Other students had been out of school for several years and were now back as part of a welfare training initiative. These students did not expect to be spending ten to twelve hours at day at the school, and MacKenzie's course load was much more than what these students had experienced in high school. They were also unprepared for the commitment required by the school, the intense hours of practical training, and the nights of clinical work at the drop-in massage clinic. These conditions led to a second narrative invented and reinforced by students: *You basically sell yourself to the program for two years. Make sure you tell your family not to expect to see you and that when they do, you'll be moody and not very friendly. The course instructors won't tell you the amount of work required because they want you to register. But once you're in, then the work piles up.*

Third, MacKenzie's students were not prepared for the psychological difficulties related to the physicality of the massage classroom. New recruits were not told that they would be required to disrobe in front of their peers, and the school offered little guidance or support for this part of the curriculum. The school did not even have hooks, hangers, divides, or places to put clothing during the practical sessions; students simply threw everything on the classroom floor. In addition to the lack of physical supports, students were not given adequate emotional support to deal with the anxieties, problems, discomfort, and emotional stress the classroom often caused. The school's official narrative, reinforced by instructors, told students to "get over" issues of body image and body-work. The students found that this official narrative was cruel and contrary to the school's mission and goals and the emerging profession of massage therapy. This led to a third student narrative about MacKenzie: *Yeah, it's embarrassing, but we all did it, and eventually it's not a big deal anymore.*

Fourth, though students did know about the school's drop-in clinic, they were inadequately prepared for the offensive situations they would face in the clinic. Since the school did not have a sexual harassment policy, students were uninformed about official recourse they could take against offensive clients, and many students were ill-prepared for their first encounter with problematic clients. In fact, the students joked about the inevitable problems faced in the clinic, and these jokes became one of the defining narratives of the clinic, leading to a fourth student narrative: *Keep the door open and make sure there is a guy [male] here when you're working. Always make sure there are two people in the area when you're working clinic.*

The students' discourse constructed the school as a dangerous, uncaring, unsympathetic environment where students had to group together to protect each other from course loads, teacher expectations, administrative blunders, and an unruly public. This narrative told students to ignore the inevitable personal difficulties and anxieties faced during class because many more encounters and problems awaited them in the clinic. However, if they could survive the two years, they would probably get a fun job. Some students even got jobs on cruise ships or at international resorts.

After completing my research at MacKenzie, it was evident why students were rebelling against the school's authority. The students' negative behaviors were indeed acts of resistance against the dominant culture at the school. But what the students did not understand—and what researchers who put too much emphasis on agency often miss—were the ways the students' own discursive structures played a significant role in reproducing the school's repressive organizational culture. The students' own discursive structures further created and reinforced the school's larger organizational culture as repressive, antagonistic, and hostile. The discourse had "stacked the deck" against the students and left future students isolated from faculty and unprepared for the problematic experiences they would face. The organizational discourse perpetuated student isolation, anxiety, and the adversarial relationship between the students and the school's faculty.

The issues of chapter 3—for Access, Penny's, Ophir, Mercur, and myself as a researcher—became how one finds agency in the face of finite structures. In this story of MacKenzie College, I would like to frame the issues a little differently. Rather than looking at agency, at MacKenzie, I needed to know how to rewrite the discursive structures that construct an organization. Working with Neil, I needed to introduce a new language throughout the organization that would put in place a new organizational culture. As the school's culture began to transform, we could anticipate that student and faculty behaviors would also begin to change. To conclude this chapter, I will briefly present some of the ways Neil and I attempted to introduce this new discourse and this new structure.

As a first-stage solution to the problems facing MacKenzie College, Neil and I decided to produce a student handbook that would introduce students to the culture of massage therapy and to the educational experiences they were about to undertake at MacKenzie. The data for the handbook would come from our joint interpretation of my research notes and from Neil's input, what he thought the school needed to turn around. Working together, we decided that the student handbook would initiate changes in MacKenzie's dominant organizational culture. We told ourselves that we were going to change the current antagonistic structure into a more student-centered, empathic, and helpful structure. We wanted the handbook to start a period of reconciliation where the narratives the students received at the school would ultimately begin to match the empathetic, healing, and cooperative narratives told by the wider field of massage therapy. In short, we wanted the school's narratives to match the images of the field we saw projected by other practitioners, associations, and massage therapy schools. Specifically, the student handbook became a device through which the school could (1) prepare students for the difficult experiences they would encounter; (2) require instructors and staff to adhere to common institutional practices that would help and support the students; and (3) protect the students from harassment, embarrassment, and other potentially harmful experiences they might face during their time at the school.

Titled *Building a Professional Community,* the handbook contained five sections:

1. A Guide to Achieving Our Professional Community
2. Achieving Professionalism and Community Through Our Mission
3. Maintaining Professionalism and Community
4. Practicing Professionalism and Community
5. Personal Issues of Professionalism and Community.

Each section described the school as a community of learners and established professional responsibilities for students who chose to become part of this community. Each section also walked students through important information they would need in order to succeed at the school. The student handbook documented the school's official policies regarding attendance, examinations, rewriting failed assignments and exams, anticipated work load, and required hours in classes and in the clinic. The handbook also explained important policies regarding sexual harassment, equal opportunity, and discrimination. At the same time, the handbook addressed the unique difficulties the students would face during their time at MacKenzie.

As the titles of these sections indicate, the handbook was written to emphasize professionalism and community, seeing the two concepts as mutually supporting and defining. "Professionalism" is typically seen as an occupational process through which people become experts in selective, specific knowledge and then use this expertise to command elite economic and social positions in society. By teaching students that they must consciously create a professional community through both the stories they tell and the ways in which they tell these stories (their dress, language, appearance, hygiene, conduct), the handbook began to establish standards for professional conduct, and it established community-regulated expectations for professionalism. Our goal was to introduce narratives that build a learning culture: students would expect to learn how to act like professionals, and simultaneously, they would learn how to regulate each other's professional conduct. From here, we hoped that the students would begin to put in place a culture of professionalism that would eventually extend into each facet of their student experience.

This is not the place to review the entire student handbook. However, three short sections are worth reproducing to help illustrate the new narratives we created at MacKenzie College: "Facilitating Professionalism," "Maintaining a Harassment Free Environment," and "Setting Boundaries: Knowing and Respecting Our Limits."

Facilitating Professionalism

This section was designed to address the many behavioral problems MacKenzie had faced. However, rather than list a coercive checklist, the handbook establishes professional goals for the student. Figure 4.1 presents the first page of this section. The next three pages of the report elaborate on each aspect of the pie chart (public, school, yourself) and discuss ways to develop a professional

Facilitating Professionalism

You are about to embark on professional training. This means that throughout this course, you are an apprentice to the profession of massage therapy and you will represent this school both on and off campus. You will also represent the profession of massage therapy in your activities in class, in the clinic, and when you practice massage in your own time.

As a successful massage therapist, you will have the opportunity to develop the respect of the public you work with. As a responsible, professional massage therapist, you must return that respect to your school, your community, and yourself. It works like the pieces of a puzzle: if one piece is missing, the picture is incomplete.

In this section, we will discuss ways for you to develop your professionalism by respecting yourself, your school, and the public you serve.

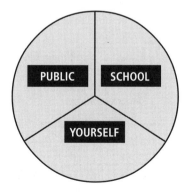

Fig. 4.1. Achieving professionalism and community: Facilitating professionalism. From *Building a Professional Community,* MacKenzie College Student Handbook.

stance within these components. In the section "Respecting the Public," students are told that "all people, regardless of their gender, sexual orientation, level of physical or mental ability, religion, political beliefs, or racial or ethnic origin, have equal right to receive massage therapy." Through the school's harassment policy, students are told that "they will be working with a broad cross-section of the public." This prepares students for their clinical work and begins to initiate them into the organizational culture MacKenzie hopes to build. This section also informs students that in order to represent the school professionally, they must be concerned about the ways they represent the clinic to the public.

The report continues in sections dealing with "respect for the school" and "respect for yourself" (see fig. 4.2). These sections follow a pattern as each section argues that acceptable behavior is a choice students will make because they want to develop a professional image as massage therapists and join the community of massage therapy.

Maintaining a Harassment Free Environment

As I noted previously, MacKenzie's massage school did not have a sexual harassment policy, even though some students had faced sexual harassment during their apprenticeship. The handbook pre-

---

When working at the MacKenzie school, we ask that you

- leave alcohol, drugs, or other potentially disruptive substances at home

- be aware of any limitations that might restrict you from providing effective treatment. These could include contagious illnesses, colds, cuts, or other conditions that may put your patients at physical or emotional risk

- present yourself to the public in a manner consistent with the professional health care community that you represent

- maintain a clean, safe, and attractive working environment for the public—if you must smoke, do so in designated areas

---

Fig. 4.2. Achieving professionalism and community: MacKenzie College policy statement. From *Building a Professional Community,* MacKenzie College Student Handbook.

sented a new policy that enabled students to take charge of their environment with the full support of the school. This policy was part of the contract the handbook established with the students. The contract states that if the students agree to act responsibly and professionally, they will have the support responsible professionals have. Figure 4.3 presents this new policy.

The policy is presented both theoretically and pragmatically. The emphasized commands "stop," "inform," "ask," "report," and

---

Maintaining a Harassment Free Environment

As part of our responsibility to our public, our colleagues, our school, and ourselves, we will not tolerate any form of personal and professional harassment.

The MacKenzie School promotes a positive policy of learning and practicing massage therapy in an environment free from discrimination and harassment. In addition to enforcing policies mandated by the ——— Human Rights Commission and the standards established by the Occupational Health and Safety Act for a harassment-free workplace, we require all of our students, instructors, administrators, and clients to treat each other with the highest standards of respect and integrity.

If, at any time, you feel uncomfortable performing or receiving a massage because of harassing conduct by a patient, student, or instructor, you must

STOP	the treatment
INFORM	the person why their behavior is unacceptable
ASK	the patient to leave the clinic (in a clinic environment)
REPORT	the incident to an appropriate supervisor
RECORD	the incident in your daily log

If you are uncomfortable with someone's conduct, it is important that you discuss this with an appropriate teacher or administrator. Teachers or administrators, who receive complaints, will

- react to complaints with seriousness and confidentiality
- document their own actions and discuss these with the person bringing the complaint
- maintain confidentiality and not seek reprisal because of any complaint
- take appropriate complaints to the necessary authorities

Fig. 4.3. Achieving professionalism and community: Maintaining a harassment free environment. From *Building a Professional Community,* MacKenzie College Student Handbook.

"record" give the students immediate responses to threatening situations and require them to challenge offensive behavior. The instructions to administrators and teachers were designed to create a contract between students and staff that outlined supervisors' responsibilities and demonstrated to the students that their concerns are important and will be engaged. Again, the policy was part of the new story of professional responsibility and accountability we hoped would take hold at the school.

Setting Boundaries: Knowing and Respecting Our Limits

"Setting Boundaries" attempts to teach students how to alleviate the anxiety associated with MacKenzie's body-work, responding to the students' concerns about removing their clothing in class, touching and being touched, and the physical discomfort associated with learning massage therapy (see fig. 4.4). The section introduces the notion of "boundaries" and associates this notion with the more common term "personal space." I hoped the manual would emphasize individual participation and individual consent by arguing that each student must be aware of his or her boundaries and must consciously act to create an environment that will be comfortable and suitable for learning massage. The section challenges students to find ways to safely expand and test their boundaries and to work together as a group to achieve a secure learning environment.

In addition to starting a conversation about personal and psychological comfort, "Setting Boundaries" also tells students about the kinds of activities they will be expected to undertake once enrolled in the college. By doing so, this narrative also becomes a screening or gatekeeping device, potentially dissuading students who may be unwilling to participate in the clinic's activities. As a gatekeeping device, the narrative develops an intentional ethos that helps to create and sustain the emerging culture at MacKenzie.

For example, the narrative uses words like "intimacy," "protection," "comfortable," and "experience" to create an image of the clinic and the people who work at MacKenzie. Words such as "feeling," "listening," "explaining," and "understanding" are used to present specific methods and approaches that students should emulate. Finally, the narrative's tone, its direct reference to the

Setting Boundaries: Knowing and Respecting Our Limits

Your boundaries are the lines you draw between yourself and other people around you. Since massage and hydrotherapy require intensive body-work, you will find that your boundaries will change considerably throughout your time here. Sometimes described as "personal space," your boundaries are physical, emotional, and psychological. While it is easy to demonstrate a physical boundary (have someone walk toward you until you become uncomfortable), it is harder to realize and understand your emotional and psychological boundaries. However, these issues are essential to massage therapy, and you will inevitably encounter times when your boundaries or your patient's boundaries will be tested and may need to be safely altered or overcome.

Your boundaries provide you with a sense of intimacy and a sense of protection. These are important and necessary, since they also allow you to judge what you are comfortable with and what makes you uncomfortable. In massage, it is important that you feel able to say no and have your feelings respected. At the same time, it is also important for you and your fellow students to create an environment where you will feel comfortable and able to experience massage, view and touch your body, and view and touch your colleagues' bodies in a safe, therapeutic environment.

In order to help facilitate a comfortable environment for you and your colleagues, you will need to place a high value on listening, talking, explaining, and understanding. Rather than rushing into an activity, be sure to discuss what you are about to do with your partner or your group. Ask your partners' permission to touch them, and explain to them what you are doing and why. After treatment you may want to talk to your partners to receive feedback, to allow them to express their feelings, and to allow them to reconsider or reposition their boundaries.

It is important to remember that boundaries are not immovable or static. They are pliable and flexible. What may be comfortable one day may be unusual or frightening another day. Again, be sure to talk about your feelings with your colleagues and allow your partner the opportunity to reposition a boundary before you begin body-work. By listening and sharing, you will develop the trust that is necessary to overcoming restrictive boundaries.

Finally, look around your classroom and invent ways to make it more secure for people to expand and test their boundaries. Again, the classroom is your space in which to grow and learn. Feel free to work with your colleagues and your instructors to create an environment in which you will feel safe and comfortable and where you will be able to take risks in an atmosphere of mutual respect and trust.

Fig. 4.4. Personal issues of professionalism and community: Setting boundaries. From *Building a Professional Community,* MacKenzie College Student Handbook.

reader ("you"), its imposition of specific emotions onto the reader, and its numerous commands tell the students that they will experience difficulties throughout the apprenticeship. By situating the reader as someone who will encounter problems, the narrative forewarns students while socializing them within MacKenzie's therapeutic educational culture.

The completed student handbook was distributed to all of MacKenzie's massage therapy students, to all incoming massage students, and to all of the school's instructors and staff. In addition, the handbook was included in recruitment materials MacKenzie College sent to prospective students.

Politics and Educational Change

I would like to frame the conclusion to this story of change in higher education in two ways. First, I would like to examine the power relations that informed my encounter at MacKenzie College. Second, I would like to return again to the larger debate about educational change in higher education in North America.

Power Relations and MacKenzie's Student Handbook

First, when one asks who wrote this story of change, it is important to note that the handbook was not developed in isolation and then imposed on the school. Although I wrote the handbook, it was a collaborative product that emerged from interviews with students, faculty, and administrators, from student comments and reviews, and from focus group interviews and tests. The handbook was also strongly influenced by Neil and his experience as the school director. I was ultimately responsible for the content and delivery of the handbook. But, rather than create a generic product that could be sold to many different organizations (a practice that is common in the consulting industry), I relied on the data collected from the narratives at MacKenzie to write a solution that was unique to MacKenzie and targeted at MacKenzie's specific needs.

Although the handbook was produced in collaboration with MacKenzie's students, faculty, and administrative staff, I later realized that the implementation of this project was not collaborative enough. The handbook received a lukewarm reception and took some time to take root within the narrative structures of the college. To some extent, this was because I did not think to include the handbook's implementation as part of my contract with MacKenzie and because the college's administrators were not willing to extend my contract to include something they assumed would not be problematic. But before getting to the handbook's reception, it is important to discuss some of the contextual events that surrounded the handbook's introduction.

Once I completed the project and delivered the student handbook, my work with MacKenzie was officially done. Approximately six months later, Neil voluntarily left MacKenzie College for family reasons. He was replaced by one of the program's full-time instructors, Amy. For the next six months, Neil acted as a consultant, helping Amy from a distance. In my intermittent conversations with Amy and Neil over the next year and a half, they reported that the handbook had been introduced at a crucial time in the college's history. Amy noted that when Neil took over as director, the school was a "train wreck." Neil was able "to get the train back on the rails," but Amy was left with "severely damaged cars."

Amy reported that she had implemented the handbook by simply giving it to students, faculty, and prospective students. The enrolled students had received the handbook midway through their course work. These students had rejected it because it was not punitive enough, arguing that the handbook did not establish enough rules and procedures, did not create ways to affix blame to specific people, and was not tough enough on people who violated college requirements. Thus, from the students' experience, in its first six months at the college, the handbook could be considered a failure. It was not received well, it was not read by instructors, and the students thought it was "soft."

However, as Foucault would note, we should not have expected anything different. The problem was that the handbook introduced a "complete discourse" that was positioned in direct opposition to the existing discourses already in place at MacKenzie. Where the existing discourse wanted revenge and blame, the handbook narrated forgiveness, professionalism, and learning. Where the students wanted punishment, the handbook talked about responsibility.

Thus, even though the existing discursive structure was creating the very things that were destroying the school, the students, faculty, and staff were still part of that structure and could not see or interpret the world according to the new discourse. Our first mistake was to ignore the ways we were going to introduce the new culture at the school. Our second mistake was to introduce the discourse as a complete whole rather than piece by piece, introducing it slowly, until it could displace the older, damaging narratives.

But Amy did not give up on the new handbook. In her next six months, she hired three new instructors and used the handbook as a central recruitment device. She reported that she asked candidates about the vision presented in the handbook and whether or not they could participate in that vision. In addition, Amy noted that she continued to distribute the handbook to incoming students, and she started testing students on their reading of it. She assigned weekly readings from it and asked students to write "reflections" on the material they read.

After a year of ideological battling over terms, procedures, and what Amy called "the approach" introduced in the handbook, two instructors left MacKenzie College. Amy replaced them, using the handbook as a touchstone to screen the new candidates. Amy reported that she also continued to use it in courses and to test students on their weekly readings from it.

Eighteen months after the introduction of the handbook, Amy started to see some significant changes at MacKenzie College. She said that the college was moving from a "rules-based culture" to a "principles-based culture." She reported that a year before, the tensions in the college had been so significant, and the culture had been so angry, few people were willing to take on the discourse offered in the handbook. Instead, students and instructors remained within their own separate narratives of "blame" and "retribution." However, as more students began their apprenticeship with an intensive reading of the handbook, and as more instructors were hired who agreed with its narrative, the college's culture began to reflect the discourse written by the handbook. Over time, MacKenzie's new narratives were realigning themselves with the college's professed image. The school's culture was beginning to change.

A year and a half after its introduction, the handbook was finally seen as part of the culture of the college, and it established the principles by which the college functioned. In my last conversation with Amy, she said that the college had finally reached a point where its members' actions were informed by a common understanding of professional community behavior rather than a strict adherence to arbitrary rules. Referencing her earlier comments about the school's "train wreck," Amy noted that the "train is finally starting to move."

Once the handbook began to take root within MacKenzie's organizational culture, Amy started writing supplementary materials based on the principles established in the handbook. In other words, she began to transport the narratives in the handbook to other written contexts throughout the school, institutionalizing the new culture at the college. Amy claimed that the college had "begun to live, demonstrate, and model" the story created by the handbook. For the past year and a half, the handbook presented a distant and ideal condition that had very little in common with the dysfunctional crisis in which it was introduced. However, by using the handbook as a guidepost and a reference, it slowly gained more prominence and relevance for day-to-day operations at the college. In this way, the handbook acted as a device through which the college could repair its dysfunctional culture and restore its identity.

As a narrative, the handbook played an important role at the school. Throughout my discussions with students, instructors, and administrators, I discovered that the school did not have a defining narrative, a story that could pre-interpret student experience. What I mean by "pre-interpret" is a way of interpreting an event before that event takes place. MacKenzie's teachers and administrators knew that their curriculum was difficult and, at times, could even be traumatic; they failed when they did not recognize that they needed to anticipate how students would react when they encountered these difficult aspects of the curriculum. Otherwise, the students had no interpretive structures through which they could make sense of their experiences. MacKenzie needed to anticipate that students were going to have serious problems in their classes; that they would attempt various ways of resisting, avoiding, and rebelling when asked to do things that made them uncomfortable; and that they would ultimately invent stories to justify this resistance, avoidance, and rebellion. This was a clear case of management assuming that because they were not communicating to their students, these stakeholders were not receiving information. However, in the absence of managerial communication, the students invented their own narratives that came to define MacKenzie's school experience. And slowly, these narratives were destroying the school.

By creating a new organizational narrative and placing this narrative ahead of the students' experience, we attempted to filter that experience through the story. Obviously, it was still going to be traumatic to take off one's clothing during class. Students were still going to create resentment when they hurt each other. The clinic was still going to be a potentially risky place. However, by pre-interpreting these events, the students would be able to anticipate what emotions and feelings they might experience and then create interpretive accounts in relation to the pre-existing narrative. The pre-existing narrative gave students the tools they needed to deal with the situations they were about to encounter.

The narratives we provided were designed to establish a context for the students' experience and to help the students situate themselves within that context and then make conscious, informed decisions about how they would react to the situation. The narratives also established a chain of accountability students could turn to when problems did arise. It is important to realize that this act of communication had significant ethical consequences. We were knowingly interpreting potentially traumatic situations for vulnerable people and were not giving these people the free opportunity to experience these situations fully for themselves. We consciously took away some of these students' agency. At the same time, we were preparing students for risky, potentially scarring events. Learning massage necessitates certain unavoidable situations, and we would be committing a greater offense if we did not prepare students for these events by implementing some kind of structure.

Stepping back from the ways these narratives influenced each individual student, it is important to note the role a central narrative had in restructuring the organizational relations at this school. The new narrative we created was designed to compete with and displace the antagonistic narratives created and employed by students and instructors in the void left by the lack of a central narrative. This was not a situation in which competing narratives were acceptable or encouraged. As such, those instructors who could not adopt the new story eventually left the school. Thus, some people profited from our change, and others lost. Were those instructors who lost unfairly treated? Could we have introduced change without creating a win/lose situation? I don't know. The instructors who left were unwilling to adopt the new knowledge and the new culture introduced by the handbook. As a result, they were replaced with instructors who were willing to support the new operating principles at the school. As Foucault noted, in contexts of change, old discursive structures are erased by the new discourse. Each organization is a constant site of discursive struggle. But in the midst of this struggle, the organization must recognize and assert its core narratives. Employees must learn these core values and decide if they can adopt them for themselves and their own work.

To some extent, the process whereby these instructors left MacKenzie is similar to what happened at Access, and it again demonstrates the weakness inherent in strong claims about agency and resistance in contexts of organizational change. People cannot act exclusively outside of organizational structures and still hope to benefit from those same structures. But I hope that our process at MacKenzie was different from the process at Access and the processes Gee, Hull, and Lankshear claim are so prevalent in "fast capitalism." At MacKenzie, we did not force an arbitrary structure on the instructors who ultimately left. These instructors were involved in the process of creating a new culture at the school. However, it should be noted that they benefited from the culture that was hurting the college and the students. The old culture of blame did not require instructor diligence, it did not require the instructors to take an active interest in the personal and professional lives of students, and it did not require the instructors to be accountable for the ways their actions contributed to the larger problems at the school. In short, the old culture allowed these instructors to believe that they were not part of any larger organizational culture. But even though they thought they were not part of MacKenzie's culture, they still played a significant role in forming and reinforcing the organizational practices at the school. As a consequence, MacKenzie resisted asserting its core values, and I believed that the competing narratives performed by these instructors were corrupting the integrity of the school.

This is not to argue that MacKenzie should or could have only one dominant narrative. Once it had repositioned and strengthened its core narrative, MacKenzie would still host many competing narratives. However, from my perspective as a consultant, as long as the core narrative we were writing was supported and reinforced both internally and externally, competing narratives could only operate as corrections and potential statements of accountability and resistance. If the core narrative was no longer supported— for example, if instructors no longer treated students with respect, or if students rejected the instructors' authority—then the competing narratives could gain ground and potentially displace our new narrative.

Competing Narratives and Change in Higher Education

Why does a book advocating university/community partnerships embark on its course by retreating (again) to school? Perhaps this constitutes a false start. Perhaps this is an admitted weakness, an unwillingness to leave my familiar terrain of education. Or, perhaps there is another more deliberate story here. If we pull our frame of reference back, we can see that MacKenzie College is only one part of a larger debate about the role higher education should play in the twenty-first century. The principal advocates of change in higher education have argued that today's system is unaccountable, outdated, and no longer capable of graduating students into viable careers and positions of leadership. For example, Ralph Lewis and Douglas Smith, in their book *Total Quality in Higher Education,* cite "the changing needs of today's economy" to argue that stakeholders outside the university's walls are pointing to a lack of quality in university education. They argue that universities are ignorant of global economic changes and that educators are unable to prepare students for life outside the academy. Lewis and Smith write: "Today's students expect of colleges and universities what they demand elsewhere: better service, lower costs, higher quality, and a mix of products that satisfy their own sense of what a good education ought to provide. They want the enterprises that serve them to be efficient—not for efficiency's sake, but because efficiency promotes the flexibility and adaptability they see in the marketplace."[16]

Sam Davis and Jim Botkin echo Lewis and Smith's criticisms of university education, arguing that "school systems, public or private, are lagging behind the transformation in learning that is evolving outside of schools, in the private sector at both work and play."[17] Davis and Botkin claim that schools have fallen behind, not just in teaching skills and aptitudes but also in preparing students for "lifelong learning," defined as a willingness and desire to continuously learn and improve. They argue that schools do not teach students to innovate, to take risks, to explore relationships between industry and education, or to view competition and rivalry as a way to evoke the best from themselves.[18] Similarly, Thomas Moore, former dean of the Arthur D. Little School of Management, argues that universities have not specialized enough to create quality programs in specific fields, that generalist faculty create nondescript, self-interested educational material that has little relevance to the outside world, and that distinct departmental and disciplinary boundaries have impeded opportunities for real learning.[19]

What these critics of higher education are capitalizing on is the lack of a strong organizational narrative in many of our colleges and universities. Like MacKenzie, too many schools believe that because they are in the business of teaching, they do not need to foster internal narratives or monitor the ways their external constituents talk about them (their image). However, as this very short review demonstrates, the discursive structures of education are vulnerable because educators have not spent enough time investing in their discourses or telling their narratives. Why do people choose to be teachers? Why has someone chosen to be part of a university? What stories does a university tell? What value does a university department bring to a student's life? What value does a university bring to its community?

It is not by accident that many of those who are most critical of university education have begun to impose the discourse of business management—specifically of "quality"—onto university contexts. These writers are seeking narratives that explain what a specific school does well and what students who attend that school can expect to accomplish and learn. By emphasizing economic principles, efficiency, "Total Quality Management," and other forms of business narratives, proponents of change in higher education have begun to draft these new discourses onto the culture of higher education—and, these new discourses are having an effect. More and more students are viewing themselves as "clients" and "customers" of universities. Courses and degree programs compete in the institution's educational market, administrators view students as "goods" that are "sold" on the market to investors (corporations), research and faculty reputations have become "value added investment drivers," scholarships are "price discounters," and student enrollment is now known as the institution's "annual yield."

Unfortunately, this has happened without a full archaeology of the new educational/business discourse. And, because we have been unable to articulate the structural transformation of educational discourse, we have been left unable to respond to this new discourse. Although many academics have argued against this marriage of business and educational discourse, few have investigated the operations that have given rise to it. What discontinuities in the discourse of education have enabled this new discourse to emerge? What events, what theories, what knowledge have allowed business discourse to displace existing discourses of higher education? How might one trace the creation of this new discourse? What transformations have occurred because of the new discourse?

I believe that it is not enough to simply refuse the new discourse. Such a refusal would leave us with nowhere to stand. Like Foucault's "man," many of our familiar educational discourses have already been washed away. They no longer hold meaning as part of education's discursive structure. Thus, before we jump to action/agency, we need to better understand the new discursive structures that are constructing education. We need to investigate the layers of this discourse, its rules, its correlations, its directions. We need to read this new discourse for its discontinuities, its contradictions, and its stumbles. Only then can we use our understanding to find new ways to subvert this discourse.

At the same time, we need to learn from this discourse, and we need to learn to change. We need to learn how to demonstrate that what happens at a university is valuable. We need to show people like Davis and Botkin that our schools have value, that our curriculum is powerful, and that our students are enabled and ready to take leadership positions. We need to do this in public environments: in magazine articles, newspaper stories, web pages, and popular books. We need to produce narratives that are compelling, inspiring, and, perhaps most importantly, accessible. This is a theme that I will return to in the book's final chapter, where I discuss specific ways universities can reconstruct their narratives and tell their stories to a wider audience. I believe that such work is vital to the future of an excellent higher education system. If those of us who believe in higher education do not produce the narratives that build up and sustain our educational structures, other people will start telling our stories for us. Once this happens, we will have little choice but to watch as the ebbing tide dissolves the grainy image of our ruined sanctuaries.

5 ▪ IMAGE: POWER, RHETORIC, AND CHANGE

> The wind was persistent now, a steady urgency upon his straight back, smoking up the dust from the road along the walk, lifting it and carrying it out to the prairie beyond. Several times Brian stopped: once to look up into the sun's unbearable radiance and then away with the lingering glow stubborn in his eyes; another time when he came upon a fox-red caterpillar making a procession of itself over a crack that snaked along the walk. He squashed it with his foot. Further on he paused at a spider that carried its bead of a body between hurrying thread-legs. Death came for the spider too.
> —W. O. Mitchell, *Who Has Seen the Wind*

Canadians and Elections

It was February on the Canadian prairie. The average daily temperature had not risen above minus forty degrees for six dark days (past the point where centigrade and Fahrenheit blend into a single, miserable cold), and the wind chills had forced mercury across the region to hide deep inside thermometers. Driving alongside my city's frozen river, I had some doubts about this next project. David, a small business success story who had become somewhat of a business mentor to me, suggested that I stop by to meet someone who wanted to run for office in an anticipated upcoming federal election. David said that she was a great candidate, just what our community needed; however, she lacked campaign experience and wanted someone to direct her media and public relations efforts. David was a talented entrepreneur and a keen supporter of my small business, and he noted that volunteering for a winning political candidate might help me attract clients and build my profile. It seemed like another lifetime since my last political campaign, but I was curious, suspiciously curious.

I was starting to learn about the history and political makeup of my new home on the Canadian prairie. One thing I quickly learned was that in the Canadian West, there is little difference between history and politics. The city had been founded in the late 1800s when the Canadian government agreed to a hundred-year contract with a group of religious folk who wanted to establish a temperance colony in western Canada. The feds gave the colony the east side of the river to be their sanctuary. I'll give the town the pseudonym Rivertown, but to demonstrate the prevalence and currentness of history here, I should note that the town's two main streets, Temperance and Colony (actual names), still exist and now are among the more chic places to live on the east side.

Residents of the east side would experience the introduction of the automobile, the enfolding of Rivertown into the expanding, surrounding city of Waterview (the west side), the beginning and the end of the Cold War, and the rise and fall of new Coke before they could legally buy a drink on this side of the river. However, as Marx's dialectic would have it, the righteous socialism of Rivertown soon gave rise to quite a different community on the other side of the river. In Waterview, the railway soiled its way through town, cultivating all the things Canadian National Railway wages could buy and all the things a temperance colony was hoping to avoid when it rose up in the middle of an isolated prairie whose tiny growing season, average daily winter temperature, and proximity from the rest of the world had successfully repulsed even the heartiest settlers.

Canadians can sense an election like a pointer senses prey: minutely at first, with slight twitches around the nose, then more dramatically, until the scent is intoxicating. This time, the scent pointed to June. In accordance, an unprecedented five political parties were selecting candidates, forming policies, and raising money as they waited for what Canadians call "the writ" to drop. Unlike our neighbors to the south, whose federal elections occur on regular and fixed dates, Canadian election dates are chosen by the incumbent prime minister, who, if part of a majority government, has the right to select a time more advantageous to the governing party than to opposition parties. For example, if after three or so years in government, the opposition parties are in complete disarray and the current government is enjoying the benefits of a strong economy and a happy populace, the country can usually expect an election call. On the other hand, if the economy is drying up, unemployment is high, and opposition politicians outnumber government members at media barbecues, government members will collect every possible paycheck until the last minute of their five-year term.

Canadians pride themselves on their political savvy and their almost genetic disposition for politics. Stop by a Tim Horton doughnut shop, a downtown pub, or, for the brave, a Saturday morning midget boys' hockey game in suburban Watertown. There, amid the SUVs and belligerent parents who are convinced their five-year-old is the next Wayne Gretzky, Canadians discuss the budget deficit and debate ways to spend a still fictional surplus, ridicule the federal government for off-loading health care priorities onto the provinces, and wonder aloud if a recently announced heritage program signals a new direction in the government's national arts strategy.

But before an election can be called, each political party must hold nomination meetings to select candidates, raise campaign money, and prepare the media and the populace for the impending barrage of pamphlets, news releases, promises, and commitments. While candidates try to show that they are important by testing platforms, giving speeches, and writing letters to the editor, backroom strategists begin stoking adrenaline rushes and all-night planning sessions with even more caffeine and tobacco. Around the corner is the election, the free-for-all among incumbents, hopeful newcomers, party loyalists, and media pundits.

But all this is still a nomination campaign away. In my experience, I have come to believe that the person who is most eager to become an elected official is usually the worst person for the job; however, David insisted that Margaret had earned considerable community respect over the years by volunteering with dozens of local groups, starting several charitable projects, and maintaining a successful medical practice. Additionally, he noted, Margaret also seemed sincere about wanting to do something innovative and positive for her community.

Born in England, Margaret came to the area in 1975 to start a medical program for the province. Here, she met her husband, a native of Egypt, who had moved to the area a full decade earlier. They were married in 1978 and had two children. Margaret was an experienced physician and was able to successfully restart her practice in this outpost serving the northern edge of the city and the spattering of communities spread north from here to Redmond, about two hours away. Redmond is home to a maximum security prison, and the Redmond folk like to tell the story of how they inherited this less than auspicious attraction. According to the myth, Redmond and the province's two other large cities, Townsend and Waterview, needed to decide how to divvy-up the federal government's three largest regional development programs: the provincial government, the land grant university, and the federal maximum security penitentiary. Electing to go alphabetically, Redmond chose the jail, Townsend chose the government, and Waterview, which by that time included Rivertown, got stuck with the university.

Margaret thoroughly enjoys this story and the way it demonstrates to her the psychology of her adopted home and its deep-seeded mistrust of any kind of authority. When forced to choose company between academics, politicians, or committed felons, these farmers, small business owners, hunters, and trappers cast their lot with the ones who had been caught. This folk history is oddly relevant, though, as the riding ("district" in American parlance) Margaret was hoping to represent encompasses the northern half of Waterview, roughly one hundred square miles of farmland, several aboriginal reservations, and the southern half of Redmond. Culturally, the northern half of the riding shares very little with the southern half, and both urban areas are worlds away from the riding's rural and ethnically diverse interior.

Although inexperienced as a candidate, Margaret was not new to politics. She had run for a position in provincial government several years before but had been defeated by the socialist incumbent. Most recently, she had stood by her provincial party leader and friend, Carolyn, while the rest of the party had mutinied and deposed Carolyn from office. Margaret knew she had lost considerable currency during this ritual bloodletting, but she was committed to Carolyn as a friend and a colleague.

After a three-hour meeting with Margaret, I was impressed by her vision, energy, and excitement. Admittedly, I was also seduced by the lure of another campaign. Like extreme sports, these struggles through grassroots democracy leave a strong, powerful residue in the blood. For the record, I was batting .750, working on two successful contests before splitting (a win and a loss) in 1990 when I had worked one campaign in Toronto on weekdays and another in my hometown on weekends. Back then, I was a political junkie—an undergraduate majoring in political science. By this time, that optimistic flame had tempered. Yet I could still feel it, a glowing, forgotten ember waiting for fuel.

I agreed to help out as a "communications assistant." I would be responsible for writing letters and campaign material, visiting potential supporters and finding ways to include them in the campaign, placing ads in local media, and preparing Margaret's nomination speech. In the terms of this book, I was responsible for the official image the campaign projected. As I drove home in my frozen green Subaru, I wondered what my first task as a communications assistant or "spin doctor" was going to be. During our introductory meeting, Margaret told me that she saw herself as an outsider in what had become a party-dominated process. She had not developed a high profile within the party, she did not have any friends on the local executive committee, and she was concerned that her gender might be a problem for many party members. However, she saw this campaign as a timely opportunity to change some long-held attitudes and political practices in this riding.

Margaret wanted her candidacy to be about changing politics in the region, and she was going to run on a platform that emphasized change: creating opportunities for those who did not regularly participate in the political process, listening to voices that were rarely heard, and achieving real goals for representative accountability in the riding. Margaret talked about electronic communication links between her constituency office and several local "nodes" throughout the riding: in schools, stores, community centers, and other public places. Here, Margaret could hold electronic surveys and polls to see what her constituents thought about current issues. She wanted to establish regional input committees that would continually monitor constituent issues and keep her apprised of local issues and concerns. She also wanted to become an advocate for this economically distressed region. She talked about regional economic development, job creation, and entrepreneurship—very real issues for a community that over the past ten years had seen most of its younger generation leave for other provinces and the United States for education and employment opportunities. I found it encouraging to see someone consider public office as a way to benefit her adopted home. I was used to candidates who speculated about cabinet positions, leadership portfolios, and personal advancement, but Margaret seemed genuinely interested in her future constituents and the very real problems she saw in her community.

From my perspective (as the campaign's spin doctor), Margaret's opponent provided a stark contrast to her "campaign for change." A consummate party insider, Rex had recently placed second in a bid to become the leader of the party's provincial wing. Having come so close to victory at the provincial level, Rex thought the party owed him the nomination for this federal campaign. A high school teacher in his late fifties, Rex had three children, and his wife maintained the family's suburban home. He had worked in provincial and federal elections throughout most of his adult life and was better known for his extensive connections than his community vision, fiscal policies, or social activism. Rex was also one of the party insiders behind the political lynching of Carolyn, Margaret's friend and former leader.

Power, an Unrecognizable Phenomenon

Though we often associate power with acts of force, power can also be a subtle and often unrecognizable phenomenon. In fact, when it is working properly, power is hardly noticeable. Ever since Foucault pointed out that there is more than just an architectural resemblance between prisons, schools, hospitals, factories, and barracks,[1] our understandings of the complexity of power and of power relations have grown considerably. Whereas power has traditionally been seen as a top-down phenomenon in which the powerful dominate the powerless, power is perhaps better seen to be a much more dynamic, productive, insidious phenomenon. Viewing power as an exclusively oppressive phenomenon does little to characterize the multiple ways in which power operates. In addition, seeing power only as overt expression does not allow us to see power in its more common and more influential operations.

I agree with Foucault when he argues that "power produces; it produces reality; it produces domains of objects and rituals of truth."[2] Seeing power as a productive agent asserts a new set of relations between individuals and authority. Rather than seeing power solely in terms of oppression and domination, Foucault argued that power is simultaneously limiting and producing. Power establishes the limits through which we can know ourselves while at the same time delineating the self we can come to know. In other words, without power, there are no guidelines or devices to aid in the structuring of everyday life—without power there is only randomness. However, as power structures randomness, it also limits and constrains, dictating ahead of time what is appropriate, correct, or best.

But Foucault's view of power is controversial. For him, power comes before truth and before knowledge. We "know" something only because we consent to the authority presenting the information. Accordingly, things are not objectively true or false, and knowledge cannot exist apart from relations of power. Thus, Foucault took to writing "power/knowledge," viewing the two terms as intricately and indivisibly tied to one another. Here, human agents have little opportunity to assert themselves freely, since all activities and ideas are formed by power relations. Thus, one cannot say that power maintains structure or that power enables agency, because the line delimiting power and structure or power and agency is too thin. Power is structure and power is agency: power operates as it needs to and always according to its own self-interest.

Even resistance is formed by power. Jon Simons notes that in Foucault's view, power requires resistance in order to exist.[3] Without resistance, power becomes domination, which is a special case of egregious or especially flagrant oppression. Looked at dialectically, resistance both undermines and supports the use of power.

Resistant actions will try to bring down or stop those attempting to use power to achieve specific ends. Yet, at the same time, by focusing on a specific agent and calling that agent "powerful," the people doing the resisting at least temporarily elevate and reinforce their opponent as powerful.

This process is illustrated in a story my friend Karen St. Hilaire enjoys telling. As a journalist in New York's North Country, she reported on a protest of the Monty Python film *The Life of Brian* organized by the Bishop of Ogdensburg, New York. Accompanied by a significant group of followers and armed with signs, posters, and pamphlets, the bishop led a protest march outside the theater showing the film. Not surprisingly, the sight of a bishop parading outside a movie theater sparked considerable attention and attracted a large group of intrigued onlookers. However, much to the bishop's dismay, after watching the bishop for a while, his collected audience decided that since they were at the theater anyway, they should go and see this controversial movie. St. Hilaire argues that the film had a very successful run in the area, largely due to the publicity generated by the bishop's protest.

In this specific context, the bishop did not understand the connection between resistance and power. He did not realize that the movie did not come invested with power; it was just a movie. However, his resistance to the movie focused more attention on it and made the movie something significant, something powerful. The movie was nothing special until the bishop made it a significant issue. Then, if people were going to appreciate the bishop's message, they first had to think that the movie was powerful and influential. Had the movie not been given this stature (as power), no one would have cared about it and fewer people would have gone to see it.

When writing that prisons, schools, hospitals, factories, and barracks share common pragmatic origins, Foucault means that each of these social institutions was established to put in place specific mechanisms to ensure that those outside of normal society and those resisting power relations in society (criminals, children, the sick, the unemployed) could be normalized, or socialized, (back) into society. Thus, prison rehabilitates criminals while simultaneously warning potential offenders about the consequences of their actions; the school system educates children who have yet to be fully socialized into normal societal behaviors; hospitals rehabilitate the sick; factories and the army instill a work ethic and an adherence to social elites (managers, commanders). For Foucault, these activities share a common mandate: to normalize potentially resistant people. At the same time, following the dialectical model of power/resistance, these institutions simultaneously harbor and create resistance to power. Yet, in doing so, they support and sustain the existing power of these same systems.

Back on the Campaign Trail

Two weeks into the campaign, I started to think Foucault should have included campaigns in his list of normalizing and disciplining institutions. The party executive had selected a date and place for the nomination meeting without consulting Margaret or her team. The agenda for the evening, including an anticipated time limit on nomination speeches, was not announced, but the party's new provincial leader was promised some time to say a few words—an odd promise in the context of a federal nomination meeting. The only membership lists available to us had not been updated for three years. Margaret's opponent, Rex, was touring the riding proclaiming that a nomination meeting would be a waste of time because he thought that Margaret could never be a serious candidate anyway. To use Foucault's terms, we were being disciplined, normalized, and categorized, and we were barely out of the starting gate.

At this point, all eyes turned to the "communications guy" for a solution to the mess we were in. The way I saw it, the problems we were facing concerned our organizational image. An organization's image is what the organization sees when it looks in what I like to call "the mirror of the marketplace." In this case, Margaret's image was what the people outside of her campaign thought about her. We had no problem with our narratives (how we perceived the campaign); these were repeated daily by volunteers, by our campaign manager, and by Margaret herself. However, we soon realized that Margaret's image was being formed by Rex. To people outside the campaign, she had become a suspicious outsider, someone who was inexperienced and untested and whose loyalty to the party was uncertain.

We needed to create an image of Margaret as the "candidate for change," and we had to find a way to stop Rex from defining Margaret in the eyes of potential voters. Our campaign was taking place in the context of a nomination meeting, a peculiar part of Canadian democracy that more closely resembles the popularity contest of a high school class president than a pillar of democracy. Only party members who live in that particular riding may vote to nominate a candidate. However, anyone who lives in the riding may join the party (for a small fee), if he or she has not already joined another party, until approximately a week before the nomination. Thus, the successful candidate is usually the best-connected person who is able to sell memberships to his or her relatives, friends, friends' friends, and so on before the nomination meeting. These "nomination-members" are rarely faithful, lifelong party support-ers, and some may even end up voting for a different party in the actual federal election. However, for the purely strategic purposes of a contested nomination, candidates must recruit as many votes as possible and then make sure that their members actually make it to the meeting and vote. We saw the recruitment of these new members as our best way to respond to Rex's preemptive strike. If we could attract new people to the party, we could position Mar-garet as someone whose campaign for change would grow the party and attract a greater following in the actual election. We argued that if she won the nomination, Margaret would win the election be-cause she appealed to a larger, more diverse audience than Rex.

Our campaign was already selling memberships, and we put more resources into recruiting new members to Margaret's camp. We wanted to portray Margaret as someone who was interested in growing, expanding, and changing the party. Since the party execu-tive decided to limit notification of the meeting to a single adver-tisement in the local newspaper, I wrote a letter that personally invited all party members to the nomination meeting (see fig. 5.1). We mailed out our brochures and marketing packages and arranged nightly meetings with interested people throughout the riding.

We kept our message positive, talking about job growth, po-

Committee to Nominate Margaret Burke

On February 24th, the Party Association will be holding a nominating meeting to nominate a candidate for the upcoming federal election. As a member of the riding association, you are invited to attend and nominate our next candidate for government.

As fellow members of the riding association, we have formed a committee to nominate **Dr. Margaret Burke** as our candidate. We are a group of local professionals, farmers, homemakers, students, and small business owners, united by a concern for our families, our communities, and our province. **Margaret** will be a diligent, hardworking, and committed individual, and we **need your vote** to help us nominate her as our candidate.

The following issues are central to the future viability of our community:

- Value-added processing—keeping the wealth we produce, the taxes we pay, and the opportunities for our families right here in our communities
- Youth employment initiatives including career education—creating local career opportunities for our children
- Sustaining the integrity of our communities—fostering trust, responsibility, and support across the many different cultures in our community.

Margaret has the experience, knowledge, and ability to act on these initiatives and to represent our community in the next government.

We need your attendance at the annual meeting to support **Margaret's** nomination. We have scheduled several informal events where interested people can meet **Margaret** and discuss election issues. Please contact us, or **Margaret,** if you can make it out to meet her.

We need your vote at the nomination meeting, Monday, February 24, at 7:00 P.M. in the gymnasium at Northwood School. We'll see you there!

Fig. 5.1. Invitation letter to members of riding association. From the Committee to Nominate Margaret Burke.

litical accountability, new opportunities for our community, and Margaret's track record. We had hit back and were starting to feel the results. Over the next few weeks, our telephone polls were reporting that people had received our material and were developing a more positive image of Margaret. We were told that people respected her, found her inspiring, and liked to see a new face in the old political game. Three nights a week, Margaret met with small groups of people at supporters' homes. There, she would discuss politics, employment, local issues, and even campaign strategies. It was a great way to gain new volunteers, it gave Margaret the opportunity to meet people from all over the riding, and it taught her to think on her feet and respond to questions quickly and sincerely. It also gave us a way to spread her image throughout the party's social networks. We anticipated that people who met with her would invite their friends to a future evening event. We hoped that these meetings would build on their own successes and get Margaret's image firmly planted throughout the riding.

At the same time, these weekly meetings and face-to-face conferences were Margaret's biggest weakness. She could appear cold and distant. At times, people complained that talking to her was like talking to a cardboard cutout. I reasoned that she was trying too hard. Her intensity appeared put-on, and her medical training had taught her how to listen and observe, not how to interact and mingle. There are probably good reasons why lawyers make good politicians: they are excellent performers, orators who thrive in a contentious, argumentative situation. Margaret was used to diagnosing, prescribing, and mandating, not to having to argue a case, entertain an audience, or play for the crowd. In these situations she became wooden and would concentrate too heavily on what she was saying, and when she got nervous, she had a bad habit of emphasizing the wrong words when trying to make a point.

As the date of the nomination meeting approached, our polling suggested that the race was close, but we were slightly ahead. We had sold considerably more memberships than Rex. Our telephone polling reported a friendly membership that respected and admired Margaret. We were in the homestretch and were beginning to feel pretty confident.

Power and the Rhetoric of Image

Foucault's notions of power have been influential and have generated significant insight into what can be a rather abstract topic. But his ideas have also been controversial, and other writers have extended and contested his theories in several ways. Predictably, most critics argue that Foucault did not pay enough attention to the role of individual agents within the realm of power. Critics like Fairclough and Giddens argue that Foucault's description of power is too oppressive, too overpowering, and too closed to human action to properly reflect the real activities individual agents can accomplish within systems of power.[4] Thus, Giddens extends Foucault's work by articulating what he calls a "reconstructed theory of power," which claims that power is generated by agents "in and through the reproduction of structures of domination."[5] What Giddens means here is that power is created and reinforced when activities, routines, and belief systems are replicated in other times and places. As we saw in chapters 2 and 3, power puts into play dominant social structures. These structures become habitual and routine for people who then attempt to replicate them in other times and in different places. For example, missionaries will attempt to replicate religious structures and habits in foreign countries, teachers will try to replicate structures of knowledge in younger generations, parents reproduce their parents' values when raising a family. When a person's habits and routines become influenced by, or even become products of, external forces, individual agents become susceptible to power. Then, acts of power are unrecognized, subtle, and effective.

By replicating itself in different places, power quietly gains acceptance as something natural or normal. People simply accept these relations as if they have always been there. If those holding power are able to create conditions for acceptance, they will be able to retain their positions of privilege. However, if currently powerful agents are unable to maintain the conditions by which their power is naturalized, their status will erode and fade as new agents replace the old order with their own social infrastructures. This is where Giddens inserts agency into power's structures, arguing that agents must choose to replicate social relations in order to build and maintain power. If no one replicates domestic relations, social patterns, or local customs, there is no power. Giddens's model seems especially relevant to political campaigns. If incumbent candidates (or governments) are able to create a structural dependence—economically, socially, or even culturally—they are more likely to convince voters to return them to power. In this context, power is not so much about sheer domination (force) as it is about narcissism, the ability of powerful groups to successfully replicate themselves within economic, social, and cultural infrastructures.

But if power is about reproduction, how can one explain change? Advocates of agency, like Giddens, contend that because humans have the ability to act in rational, autonomous ways, acts of reproduction are simultaneously acts of power and acts of change. Giddens argues that "change is in principle involved with social reproduction" and again that *"change, or its potentiality, is thus inherent in all moments of social reproduction"* (emphasis in original).[6] As agents organize and interpret their lives, they simultaneously reproduce and change features of their lives.[7] Power is the force that controls this organizational and interpretive process.

But, there are several limitations here. First, and perhaps most importantly, Giddens's model assumes the primacy of agency, meaning it assumes that humans always have the capacity to act rationally and autonomously. Roy Boyne has called this "an illusory ideal for social theorists" because it ignores the connections between power and knowledge.[8] How can individuals act rationally and autonomously if what they consider their "knowledge" is actually a manifestation of power? Actions that I think are autonomous may actually be deeply connected to my church or my peer group. Humans are not wholly free agents; they are part of human society and have been influenced by human history, language, and social organization. Even those who choose to leave society are doing so because of the ways they have been influenced by society. Although these people can claim some degree of agency, they still cannot claim to be completely separate from social structures.

Second, Giddens has no justification for his assertions about human agency other than a utopian idealism, a liberal hangover, so to speak.[9] Giddens's ideal puts human agency at the outskirts of human possibility, suggesting that if we simply work hard enough, we can become what we desire. While such Platonism is inspiring, one cannot build an effective theory of social action on an illusion. By blindly assuming the primacy of agency, we unknowingly can be reinforcing the structures of power around us.

Third, social reproduction is not a sufficient factor for change. Social reproduction might bring about change, but there is no guarantee that it will. In addition, as we have seen in cases where one discourse replaces an existing discourse, change can occur indepen-

dent from or even in opposition to social reproduction. Social reproduction may explain how, in some cases, elites manage change
and still retain power. But such an explanation seems facile and
obvious. More pressing questions are: How does such reproduction
occur? What are elite strategies of power? How self-aware are
agents of power? How do people manage and direct such transformations? How do people insulate their power from others when
they are most vulnerable and weakest?

As a way to create some middle ground in the structure/agency
debate, I argue that power can be more productively seen as the self-
reflexive ability to control an image.[10] A powerful organization is
able to manufacture an external image that will stick in the minds
of consumers, competitors, and other stakeholders within the industry. Powerful people are able to control how they are interpreted
and perceived by other people. A powerful political candidate will
successfully control how the voters view not only him or her but
also competing candidates. *Image-power* is not constant but situational and highly dependent on context. It enables people to define others while resisting others' definitions of one's self. Image-
power can be fleeting and always operates in strategic accordance
within and against existing structures.

Image-power, like the organization's narrative, is a discursive
product. It is created strategically using specialized discourse, vi-
suals, sounds, and other forms of what academics call rhetoric, or
the tools of persuasion. It is formed self-consciously and self-reflec-
tively. In other words, powerful people know that they are constructing an image, and they are able to think about and monitor
the ways this image is being constructed. This self-reflection assumes
human agency and assumes that people will be able to examine and
recognize social, economic, and political structures. Moreover, it
also assumes that people will be able to see how they are positioned
according to the structures around them. This is an assumption I
am willing to grant, since self-reflection seems to be a meeting point
between structure and agency. Self-reflection is structural in that it
must be learned, practiced, and socialized. At the same time, self-
reflection is an act of agency as it enables the person to see how
actions, beliefs, and motives are influenced by structure.

But image-power is not only about reproducing social structures; it is also about the ability to reproduce, alter, create, or otherwise influence the way other people perceive images. A powerful organization will be able to control not only the way it is perceived in the wider market but also how other companies in the same market are perceived. A weak organization will be subject to the images constructed for it by more powerful players. Therefore, in the same way that narratives compete for legitimacy within an organization, images compete for legitimacy outside the organization. This is why a political campaign is such a rich terrain for the rhetoric of image. It is the discursive process of the market forced into a few short months. Candidates have little time to generate an image that will stick with as many voters as possible. At the same time, competing candidates are trying to generate and promote images of themselves and of each other. In the end, the most powerful—the one who is best able to define the campaign, the competitors, and the context—wins.

The Campaign That Never Was

Our initial strategy for Margaret's campaign was to integrate her within the riding's social infrastructure and project her as a long-time community activist and supporter. So, we spent the next month and a half setting up meetings for Margaret with potential supporters, talking policy with mayors and church leaders, and giving talks at community groups and business meetings. Margaret was tireless and remained confident. Every evening, while she met with her focus groups, volunteers would gather in the campaign's small central office to canvass the existing membership, call supporters, and remind people to attend the nomination. We would speculate about our support and write and rewrite campaign material. The flier reproduced here as figure 5.2, which was written before I became involved in the campaign, was one of our most published and distributed pieces. In reproducing it here, I have changed identifying geographical and political information but have kept much of the original text complete.

With a week to go, new memberships closed, and Margaret and I began to work on the final draft of her speech. The party executive

From the Committee to Nominate Margaret Burke

to represent the Party for the Federal Riding of Champlain

"Living in Harmony"

In 1996, the United Nations again chose Canada as the number-one country in which to live. This is according to our high standard of living, the opportunity to become educated and to work, and the relative freedom from debilitating environmental conditions and violence.

With these as indicators, a Canadian think tank further concluded that within Canada, our province was the best place to live. Most of us would agree. Although at times we feel the heavy burden of taxes and, as our children move elsewhere to work, we feel a sense of loss, overall, there are plenty of positive benefits and obtainable opportunities to be achieved here.

The federal riding of Champlain is made up of individuals who are hardworking, tax-paying families with both parents on the job. We manage the farm, we work in home-based businesses, and we commute to our places of work in the service, industrial, and high-tech industries. All the while we are working to provide care, love, and development to our families—our children.

Champlain is made up of individuals who are progressive, diligent, and deserving. To represent this area would be a demanding but rewarding task to any individual who understands its electorate.

We believe that the issues of concern to our community involve the following:

- Agri-value and value-added business and ag-biotech industries: promotion of research and development, national and international marketing of our agricultural products
- Youth employment initiatives and youth regard
- Economic growth and continued fiscal responsibility: continued initiatives for small business
- Preservation and proper maintenance of the federal social safety nets:
  a) protection of Canadian Pension Plan contributions
  b) implementation of universal day care
  c) revision and improvement of social welfare
- Strengthening our justice system and providing more accessible social networks to eliminate violence
- Preservation and support of the family

To address these issues and to create productive results for change, we believe that Margaret has the ability to work hard with commitment, the experience to implement ideas, and the skills to bring people together toward building a better community.

Margaret has a proven record of personal success complemented by public participation that will assist her as she prepares to represent us in public political office.

Professionally

Since emigrating to Canada in 1975, Margaret has built a successful career in Redmond as a doctor. She travels extensively, conducting clinics in Northwood, Springville, and other rural communities surrounding Redmond and Waterview. She is married and has two children, aged 14 and 19.

For Our Party

Margaret was past candidate for Redmond in 1991 and is past president of the Provincial Party's Women's Commission. Since 1990, she has served as social policy chair and advisor to the Provincial Party. Margaret was chair for the subcommittee for policy on social services and the family. Margaret has also been actively involved with federal politics for the past ten years.

For Her Community

Board member	Redmond Big Sisters Organizations	1976–79
Chairperson	Family Life Committee Sacred Heart Cathedral Parish Council	1978–81
Founder	Redmond Aboriginal Boarding Home	1979
Coordinator, councillor	Trinty Television, "It's a New Day"	1979–84
Councillor	Redmond Coffee House Street Ministry	1979–83
Board member	Catholic Family Service Board	1985–88, 1995–96
Chairperson	Redmond Citizens Organized to Resist Pornography	1987-90
Chairperson	Steering committee to investigate the potential of a rehabilitation treatment center for ex-offenders	1989–90
Board member	Steering committee for alcohol and drug abuse center	1989–90
Board member	Redmond Multicultural Center	1990–97
Member	City of Redmond Elimination of Racism Committee	1992–93
Liaison officer	North American Indigenous Games Committee for Accommodations	1993
President	Save the Rail Committee	1994–95
President	Prairie International Economic Trading Foundation	1994–96
Board member	Holy Family Hospital	1996–97
Member	Redmond Chamber of Commerce	1989-97
Member	Waterview Chamber of Commerce	1997

"If chosen to represent this riding, it will be my responsibility to take your concerns, ideas, and solutions to Ottawa and bring back to the people of Champlain the assistance to obtain our goals."

—Margaret Burke

If you have any ideas, concerns, or comments about what we are presenting, please contact any of the following people: Margaret Burke at (123-456-7890) or Sandi at (098-765-4321). Thank you. You are invited to attend Town Hall meetings, held every Friday at 7:00 P.M. at 123 45 Avenue. Please call 765-4321 if interested in attending.

Fig. 5.2. Margaret's campaign document. From the Committee to Nominate Margaret Burke.

announced a maximum time limit of twenty minutes, so we knew that we would have about fifteen minutes to hold onto our supporters and perhaps even sway some of Rex's support. We sat down to the task of presenting and commodifying Margaret's image.

We had three objectives when writing Margaret's speech. First, we wanted her to appear as a natural, normal part of the community's social infrastructure. We assumed that people would be more likely to vote for someone who was like them, someone they could relate to and who shared their experiences. This required that we downplay Margaret's immigrant roots and instead focus on her quick assimilation into Canadian society. We also had to promote the significant things she had done for her adopted country: her medical practice, her community work, her involvement in local issues.

Second, we wanted Margaret to appear active and exciting, as someone who had lots of ideas, who wanted to change the riding, and who could get something done. This was easy as these issues were at the heart of Margaret's desire to run for office. She was at her best when talking about ideas for job growth and youth employment; she was excited about networking the riding and putting electronic "democracy boxes" in places where people could e-mail her and write about their problems and their ideas.

Third, we wanted Margaret to appear compassionate. We thought that a compassionate and empathetic candidate would contrast sharply with Rex's programmatic candidacy. We wanted her to show that she understood the problems people were facing and that she sincerely cared about her community's needs. Margaret was running to get an important job done, not because she wanted to be an elected official or because she thought someone owed her something.

After completing the first draft of her speech, Margaret tested it in front of a group of campaign volunteers, whose suggestions formed my second and third drafts. We then pilot-tested the speech for a variety of groups, a process that led to drafts four and five. Finally, Margaret and I sat down and polished draft six.

"Hello, I am Margaret Burke," the speech started. Then Margaret described her background:

I came to Canada in 1975, a country that the United Nations has again chosen as the number-one country to live in. I am proud of our standard of living, our opportunities to become educated and to work, and our example to the world of a peaceful, safe society.

This introduction echoed the key messages in Margaret's other campaign materials. It was conservative, positive, and of course patriotic. The speech continued:

Canada has given so much to me and my family. Over the years, we have built a successful health care practice. My husband has recently retired from a long career as a surgeon, and my children will soon be attending [the provincial] university.

Our concern going into the speech was that the audience would view Margaret as an outsider because she was not born in the area. In addition, we wanted to quickly jump to Margaret's rationale for public service. So the introduction continued:

Our lives have been richly blessed here. And now it is the time for me to give back to my community and to my province my time, my efforts, and my expertise. Now that I have been blessed with all of the opportunities this province offers, I want to use this time to devote myself to fully representing and working for you—a community that is so dear to me.

As the introduction continued, Margaret talked about her professional life and family, and then she more directly addressed her position in the riding and her status as an "outsider":

We are an eclectic and diverse people: We are immigrants, born as far away as Egypt, India, Germany, England, and Hong Kong. We are natives of this land, born into a long, proud, and historic tradition which our aboriginal ancestors have passed down to us. But no matter where we are from, our children are born in Canada, and they worry about the future of our country.

At this point, the speech made a transition to the personal and economic issues faced by people in the riding. In this section, we wanted to talk about economic issues by profiling the successes, challenges, and problems faced by real members of the community:

We are a diverse people, but in our diversity we also share many common bonds, common hopes, and common fears. As I have traveled throughout our community, I have seen our common joy when children are baptized, when Walter Field bought a new truck, when a new business is set up in Redmond, and when my nephew Donny Burke graduated from high school.

I have also experienced our frustrations and our pain: the pain our neighbors felt when their children moved away to take jobs in other provinces, the anxiety of having the bank foreclose on a small business, the frustration of back-logged grain, and the anger of not knowing when somebody in Ottawa will move a piece of paper from one side of the desk to another.

I also think of a recent conversation I had with a farmer who told me that business has been so tight lately that he could no longer meet his friends for their weekly coffee—and he couldn't afford to renew his membership in our party.

Over the years, these stories, your stories, have deeply touched me, and they have convinced me that this campaign must become a new way of doing politics. We must commit ourselves to local decision making, to listening to local authorities, and to really representing and working with our community. My candidacy can be the beginning of this new approach to government.

Margaret's use of stories, made apparent in the phrase "these stories, your stories," was, of course, a shameless link to my own research interests. But it seemed to fit, and the people we tested it on liked the stories and nodded as they recognized the various people Margaret mentioned. This section was important for other reasons as well. We needed to show that Margaret was in touch with the community, that she had deep roots here, and that she knew about the daily issues and struggles the local people faced. By personalizing these anecdotes and turning them into stories, I hoped that Margaret could become part of the community's larger social narratives.

The phrase "my candidacy can be the beginning of this new approach to government" signaled a turn in the speech towards the things Margaret wanted to stand for and what she was hoping to accomplish. These were going to be her commitments to her constituents. In my work on various election campaigns, I've noticed that politicians rarely refer to "promises" anymore. Instead, they now talk about commitments. Rhetorically, this seems to work better, but it also shows that people are increasingly cynical about electoral promises. For some reason, a "commitment" seems more durable than a promise. Yet, a commitment does not necessarily pledge action; it merely signals a trust or a desire for something. In our case, Margaret was going to "commit" to several broad issues—accountability, accessibility, and openness—and we highlighted these commitments in a pledge she made midway through the speech:

> This is the backbone of my pledge to you: If this riding that we create together is not open to new ideas, new suggestions, and new voices, if our elected representative is not accessible by every citizen of this riding, and if our representative and our party is not accountable, then we will have failed in our mission to this community.

As the speech continued, Margaret took some necessary crowd-pleasing shots at the other political parties that would eventually oppose us in the actual election; then, once the cheers and applause quieted, she said, "Let's talk about some real community issues." She listed her action plan: leadership committees in each area of the riding that would be responsible for keeping her informed of community issues; economic development plans, which she continually highlighted in her campaign documents; and increased support of agricultural businesses, chemical processing, and biological research, which would create jobs in this largely agricultural economy.

In our conclusion, we wanted to position Margaret as someone who would get things done for her community. To do this, we decided to work from the phrase "the first place people will go." Margaret pledged that her constituency office would be "the first place people will go when they need help solving a problem." Her office would become a marketing and promotional center for industry, trade, and business resources. It would be an electronic hub, networking schools, libraries, offices, and government departments. Repeating this theme, Margaret said that her office would be "the first place people will turn when they want to start a business," and she named several local entrepreneurs and businesses that served as good examples of successful family-owned enterprises.

Finally, Margaret pledged that midway through her term in office, she would hold a public review of her performance as a representative. She called this a "report card" and said that it "will enable you to evaluate my record as your representative and my office's ability to help you and help our community." This brought us to the conclusion of her speech, which again stated her commitments to community input, accountable representation, and leadership by listening.

Overall, I thought it was a pretty strong and powerful speech. It lasted exactly fifteen minutes, and the final draft was heartily endorsed each time Margaret delivered it. She had worked it into memory and seemed pretty comfortable with the whole performance. We felt ready for the big nomination.

The Nomination

The nomination was held on a Monday night in a local school gymnasium. We arrived early and decorated the walls with "Margaret" signs. We hired a violin and accordion duo to play German and Ukrainian waltzes (representing the predominant cultural makeup of the riding). When we found out that the executive committee had no plans for refreshments, we brought in two huge coffee percolators and served coffee in cups with "Margaret" stickers on them. When people arrived, they eagerly wore our stickers and asked for her promotional material. Some even waltzed up and down the aisles to our music.

Twenty minutes before the meeting was about to start, the party executive arrived and announced that in order to speed up the evening, the time for speeches was reduced from fifteen minutes to five and that Margaret would speak first. The party secretary then announced that Margaret's signs were distracting and needed to be removed from the front of the stage. The duo had to stop performing. Margaret's team was fined for serving coffee without first obtaining permission from the executive committee. We were stunned and off-balance. Margaret and I went to work gutting ten minutes out of her speech.

Rex arrived ten minutes late. He gave a halfhearted speech about his family's pioneering role in the community that lasted exactly four and a half minutes. He shook some hands, waved to the crowd, and then won the nomination by a 2-to-1 margin. In a ten-minute speech, the provincial leader congratulated "his friend" for his "well-deserved victory" and encouraged everyone to turn their attention to the federal election, after which "his friend" would become our next elected representative. The party secretary gave Rex a bouquet of roses. Rex thanked his supporters, kissed his wife, waved, and went home. He never spoke to Margaret.

The Aftermath

Margaret had insisted that her campaign was about change: changing women's roles in the community, changing the disturbing trend of declining citizen input in public decision making, changing the nature of who was heard and who was represented in government. After it was all over, we tried to understand what went wrong. Our hours of conversation, polling, and discussion told us that many of the people who voted for Rex were sympathetic to Margaret's candidacy and to the issues she raised. People agreed that the region needed more employment opportunities and that we needed more women in public office. People respected Margaret and told us that they thought she would be a good candidate. However, these same people voted for Rex. We could understand if the contest had been close, had we lost by a narrow margin. But once the results were announced, we realized that we were never even in the game.

There were pragmatic organizational issues: we were not able to get all of our members out to the nomination, the public fine made us look bad, Margaret's speech was a wash. But these issues did not account for such a large margin of defeat. People could have overstated their support to appear polite or nonconfrontational. Some people may have simply lied to us. But these explanations do not explain people's motivations, their reasons why they would not support Margaret.

Though we can never know with certainty why we were unsuccessful, I suspect that one of our mistakes involved a deep misunderstanding of what social theorists would call the "fields of power" in which the nomination process operated. In our efforts to change the social and political fabric of the district, we mistook relations of power for relations of change. We assumed that we were out to change the community when, in fact, we had launched a power struggle. Despite his unsuccessful campaign to become provincial leader, Rex was still very much a party "insider," and he was right to see this nomination as his reward for years of federal and provincial party service. As we soon found out, neither the provincial leadership nor the local party executive was terribly impressed when Margaret's campaign almost spoiled what was supposed to be a simple coronation. Despite her (our) loss, Margaret's campaign was actually more successful than it really should have been. Although she was an equally (or more) qualified candidate with an equally effective organization, Margaret really had very little chance of defeating Rex. This is not because we were unable to successfully introduce and manage change but rather because we were wrong to perceive this campaign to be about change. It was not. It was about power. Rex's candidacy was the necessary fulfillment of a regular, historic process in which a high-profile, socially conservative male from a recognized prairie family with strong party connections always won the party's nomination in this community. Margaret's candidacy challenged this strongly held tradition.

In this way, Margaret's candidacy represented a direct attack against this community's image of their leader. Yes, people agreed with us when we argued that women should play a greater role in political life in the riding, people were all in favor of expanding citizen input in the democratic process, and everyone agreed that the region needed more entrepreneurship and job creation. And, they saw Rex as just the man for the task. The predominant social image in the community still reflected a leader who was male, married (heterosexual), socially conservative, and prairie-born and raised. Our campaign did nothing to challenge this perception, to challenge the community's image of itself, or to try to displace this image with a competing one.

Ideally, we needed to demonstrate the ways in which the community's image was no longer reflected in the lives of most of its members. We needed to show that this image was contradicted by most residents' personal and occupational narratives. Such a task would have required several years of rhetorical groundwork and a much higher profile Margaret who could enter the contest with a strong existing image and an ability to maintain that image as Rex's supporters attempted to redefine and reposition her. Margaret needed to be seen years ago as a social and economic advocate. She could have produced a newspaper column, started a high-profile nonprofit organization, or been a regular commentator on radio or television. However, without this kind of image, we were instead attempting to force "difference" onto this community. We wanted people to violate deeply embedded social structures and traditions without first establishing a premise for doing so. I suspect that this is why people did not vote for us. In the end, we were not attempting to create "change"; we had instead launched an assault against the community's basic values and social structures. People were not going to elect someone to represent them if they thought that person was antagonistic to their basic social values—even if those basic values were the very things limiting their personal opportunities and destroying their community's economic infrastructure.

By unwittingly turning the campaign into a contest of power, we placed ourselves in the position of outsiders resisting and challenging the power held by party insiders. By allowing ourselves to be cast as outsiders, our arguments for change validated and reinforced Rex's dominant social position in his community. In this way, we legitimated his candidacy. This occurred in at least three ways. First, our own campaign issues marginalized us, since we identified ourselves with those out of work and out of power. As soon as we positioned ourselves as a voice for those on the margins of society, Rex could position himself as the voice of the successful, mainstream, upwardly mobile members of society.

Second, we challenged the party executive's established candidate. This was evident at the nomination meeting when the party executive publicly destroyed the image we were working so hard to cultivate. We were forced to remove our posters and fined for serving coffee, and our band was deemed inappropriate. This was an overt act of image-power as the party executive committee used their currency as existing leaders to define and characterize us as rebellious outsiders. Perhaps our best response at the time might have been to call these practices to everyone's attention. Such an action would overtly try to wrestle image-power away from the party executive. Yet, it takes an enormous amount of courage and presence to be able to attack the grounds of image-power at the moment one is subjected to it.

Third, Margaret's speech showed that she was outside the party hierarchy. Rex knew about the new time limit and came prepared with a four-and-a-half minute speech. Margaret could only further solidify her position as outsider by crying foul, formally protesting the new rules, and then appearing agitated and unprepared during her own speech. Rex needed an outsider, an opponent to resist his authority, someone to challenge him and his legitimacy so that he could display his power and his influential position as a party insider. In this community, at this time, Margaret's very candidacy assured Rex's victory.

Power, Rhetoric, and Change

I left this project feeling troubled. Certainly, Rex's supporters will call this story unfair. To use the discourse of politics, some may call it a "hatchet job." They will claim that they worked just as hard as we did, that Rex was simply a better candidate, and that they ran a better campaign. Maybe they are right. But when I ask myself who profited from my involvement in this campaign, who profits from the story I am now telling, and who loses, the answers are not that straightforward. Did Margaret benefit from my help? I hope so, but I cannot be certain. Did my community benefit? Even though we were ultimately rejected by the majority of voters, I think it is too easy to say we should not have tried. Although Margaret's campaign was not accepted by her community, by running, she made sure that the nomination would be a contest, that there would be a democratic process, and that this was not a simple coronation. By helping Margaret, we became involved in our democracy and in the political life of our community, and ultimately, I think our community profited from these activities. Who profits from this story of the campaign? This is a question readers will need to decide. Perhaps some may argue that the story's representation is a little disingenuous, that I am too kind to my own involvement and not critical enough of the work we did or the positions we took.

Looking back at this story, I think it presents several consequences for argument and argumentation that I still find troubling, because they get to the heart of what I do and what I would like to believe. I chose to study and teach communications because I believed in the concept of persuasion. I believed that language had the power to persuade other people and to create change peacefully. Following Kenneth Burke, I've taught my students to believe (at least for the duration of my courses) in something called rhetoric and that people can solve their problems nonviolently through argumentation and persuasion. I don't think I am alone here. I've read countless textbooks assuring students that a well-crafted argument can evoke alternative ways of thinking and can ultimately persuade people to adopt new ideas. As Annette Rottenberg writes, we believe that people use language to "justify what they do and think" and "to solve problems and make decisions."[11] Through argumentation, discussion, and conversation, people can learn, grow, and ultimately live together peacefully.

Such definitions and inspirational accounts are well known and often repeated in the business of teaching. Yet, in the context of Margaret's campaign, they seem naive and perhaps a little simplistic. From my perspective, Rex's victory had little to do with his rhetorical prowess or his understanding of ethos, logos, and pathos. In addition, on that night, there was no language, no heartrending speech, no passionate last-minute plea that would have persuaded our audience to vote for Margaret. No amount of rhetorical bravado would have won the day. Rex's victory was a power play, not a debating tournament.

This leads me to wonder if we are correct to assume that argument really matters in a world of power-brokering, strategic moves, and political deal-making. A good speech might receive a few laughs and a resounding applause at a wedding, but there seem to be increasingly few occasions for speech-making and argumentation in today's world. There seem to be even fewer occasions when a good speech or a great paper will play any role in solving social problems, addressing a community need, or fixing a struggling organization. Does this mean that I am doing a disservice by teaching that argument matters? Am I naive to hold out the possibility that someday people will turn to negotiation or dialogue to solve their problems? Deep down, I intuitively feel that these are still good ideals, and I don't think that we should abandon them. Like Giddens, I still hope that someday humans will strive to reach these ideals. But at the same time, such idealism needs to be brokered with a little bit of structure. We should not fall into the trap of thinking that people will always be reasonable and open to persuasion.

We need to teach argumentation, speech-making, and we need to teach rhetorical aptitudes, ways to convince and persuade. But we also need to teach "power aptitudes." We need to show how special interests achieve political goals. We need to teach communications strategy. We need to show how lobbyists work and to teach strategic sensibility, an awareness of when to argue and when argument is simply a waste of energy. We need to teach how to read a situation and determine the roles power, rhetoric, and change are playing and how strategic players may be able to influence these roles.

Postscript

In a bid to secure votes in suburban Ontario, Rex's party endorsed gun control and abortion rights legislation. Out here in the West, of course, this was the kiss of death to Rex's political aspirations, and he who lived by the party died by the party. Rex was trounced in the federal election by an even more conservative male with even deeper roots in the community.

Two months later brings late summer to the prairies. The shade of my apple tree has been devoured by hundreds of green caterpillars (saturate the tree with dish soap, the local paper suggested), and my shorthaired pointer has spent the summer taking full advantage of the long days to chase sticks in the river. From the country music station on our kitchen radio, I hear a familiar tune. I turn up the volume loud enough so I can sing without having to hear myself. Together, Tracy Lawrence and I sing an old country tune about change, permanence, and how, in a world where everything seems to be changing, it is often hard to distinguish between the two. On the surface, there seems to be some truth to Lawrence's folksy lyrics—especially here, where in a few short months the thermometer will again plunge to minus forty degrees, where our biggest export continues to be talented youth looking for work, where farmers drive brand-new pickup trucks to crop insurance offices after yet another summer drought, and where men like Rex vie for power solely because it is their prerogative to do so.

That night, my wife and I join some friends for dinner at Red Lobster. Much to everyone's surprise, I order a Budweiser to accompany my seafood. Not being much of a drinker, my reasons are entirely theoretical: an American beer in a seafood joint on the edge of an old temperance colony in the heart of the Canadian prairies. I wrap the bottle in a napkin and take it home as a personal reminder, and a symbolic testament, to agency, to power, and to change.

6 ▪ DISCORDANCE AND REALIGNMENT: STORIES FROM THE FINAL FRONTIER

> It has occurred to Ms. Mimi Adler, whom I like a lot, to wonder whether people reflexively think of their lives as stories, because from birth to death they're exposed to so many narratives of every sort, or whether contrariwise, our notion of what a story is in every age and culture reflects an innately dramatistic sense of life, a feature of the biological evolution of the human brain and of human consciousness, which appears to be essentially of a scenario-making character.
> —John Barth, *On with the Story*

> Memory is a kind of homesickness.
> —Ivan Doig, *This House of Sky*

Introducing Cemeteries and Change

A story about cemeteries must also be about death. But insofar as death is a story of permanence, it is also a story of change and transformation. The following story is about how an organization, a city-run cemetery, used its hidden stories to dynamically change itself in response to the threat of a corporate takeover. It may be difficult to correlate cemeteries, stories of death, corporate take-overs, city councils, and topics of change management. It may be difficult to see change in rows of headstones, monuments, flowers, and trees. Yet, as a story of corporate survival, this is about how the threat of takeover stimulated an organization to revive itself and create a new, dynamic corporate culture.

I became involved with Andrew and the cemetery business by listening to the stories he would regularly tell me about his world at Pleasant View. Like most people, I rarely went out of my way to attend a funeral or visit a cemetery. For me, cemeteries were uncomfortable places, and there have been times when they were downright frightening. As a teenager, I attended Halloween dances in a rural community hall whose backyard cemetery was a popular place to play midnight hide and seek. Years later, I rented a room in a house that backed on to a cemetery, but my room was in the front of the house and I deliberately used the street-side entrance. My strangest funereal experience was when my ex-girlfriend's parents gave me a brass rubbing from a medieval gravestone as a wedding present.

Over the years, though, cemeteries have become more significant and more important to me. Some time ago, I was able to visit Beethoven's grave in Vienna's Central Friedhof. The grave had been excavated and moved to the Central Friedhof in 1792. There, it became part of a composers' corner, along with the graves of Schubert, Brahms, Josef Strauss, and Johann Strauss and a monument to Mozart (whose body was lost). Despite having become a tourist stop, easily accessible by the train, the site was obviously meaningful and sacred for many people. As I read the stone inscription and watched other visitors leave flowers, candles, and handwritten notes on the grave, I could see the very real impact that Beethoven, and now this site, has had on people. More recently, I have been to a less prestigious but equally meaningful cemetery to bury my grandfather, the steelworker who taught himself how to build a dormer by tearing apart the house down the street.

But these are all more recent experiences. At the time Andrew, the director of my city-owned cemetery, asked me to help him write a five-year business plan for Pleasant View, I had never thought about a cemetery as a business, and I had a very hard time getting my mind around writing a business plan for a business I had little interest in frequenting. But the more I thought about this unique project, the more the topic grew on me.

Burton Bledstein documented that in 1860, funeral directors organized themselves from groups of trade workers into a professional community. This movement proposed the National Funeral Directors' Association, which would ensure the proper education, examination, and licensing of directors as professionals. In 1884, funeral directors adopted their first code of ethics, which boasted, "There is perhaps no profession after that of the sacred ministry in which high toned morality is more imperatively necessary than that of funeral directors."[1] Yet, as Jessica Mitford has repeatedly shown, the twentieth-century "death care" industry is better recognized for the imposition of scandalously high-priced services on a vulnerable constituency and, more recently, for the big-money, breakneck expansion of Dallas-based Service Corporation International (SCI) and the Canadian chain the Loewen Group Inc.[2]

Mitford's most recent report on SCI reveals an extremely aggressive company that, with revenues exceeding $1 billion in 1994 and $1.5 billion in 1995, has grown by purchasing local funeral homes, cemeteries, and crematoriums, effectively securing a stranglehold on many communities' death-care services. In 1997, SCI failed in its attempted hostile takeover of the Loewen Group. As Mitford notes, had SCI been successful, it would have owned over 3,700 funeral homes and "would have performed one of every seven American funerals."[3] In a practice well known throughout North America's death-care industry, both SCI and Loewen specialize in purchasing and operating reputable, family-owned funeral homes without changing the home's name or in many cases the family-based personnel. By buying several homes in one city, SCI and Loewen are able to borrow the credibility of long-term family businesses and secure the profits of operating multiple homes in one location, all the while retaining the perception of local competition among a region's death-care providers.

Emerging from this little-known backdrop was Andrew, the director of Pleasant View Cemetery, who said that a multinational company—Security Corp.—had recently offered the city $2 million for Pleasant View. Most of the city politicians did not know that the city operated a cemetery and decided that they had better learn more about this civic institution before they used the proceeds of a lucrative sale to reduce the city's debt. Thus, the city council instructed Pleasant View to submit a five-year business plan and undergo a thorough business audit so that they could determine whether to sell the cemetery to Security Corp. Andrew, a recent college graduate, had only been director at Pleasant View for six months. As he noted to me, he had little confidence in the "goodwill" of city politicians and saw this business plan as his only way to protect "the legacy of trust the city promised to generations of citizens from the onslaught of corporate expansion."

As Andrew's statement suggests, the stakes involved in this project were frighteningly high, and my role was to be anything but objective. As an academic consultant, I was intrigued with this client who was asking me to write against radical changes in this context of absolute permanence. As we worked together and as the business plan began to emerge, I witnessed and experienced the ways people use stories and myths within unstable, changing contexts, and I gained many insights that helped me see the connections and the order communication can build when our social spaces, our work spaces, and even our religious spaces become threatened.

Structure, Agency, and Change

Previous chapters have discussed the study of agency, structure, and power and the ways these concepts intersect with moments of change. Chapter 3, the story of Access Bank, introduced the concepts of habitus and routinization, taken from work by Bourdieu and Giddens. These terms describe how people's actions emerge from larger social environments and social structures. Bourdieu's concept of the habitus describes lasting and transferable attitudes and social instincts people are taught from birth. These instincts allow us to improvise social conduct in different places at different times. Our habitus makes it possible to interpret how to behave in new social situations, based on the rules of behavior we have learned from previous situations. For good or ill, we rarely think about or consciously decide how to behave in most social situations. We largely let these instincts and learned behaviors act for us.

Habitus is useful on both practical and theoretical terms as it describes and explains how people integrate themselves into society through learned but unacknowledged daily activities, habits, and routines. As Bourdieu writes, the habitus incorporates a person's aesthetic taste, clothing styles, food preferences, sports, and friends, all as objective products of social conditioning. This is not to say that the habitus structures and conforms individual behavior. Instead, it should be seen as an indication of the social structures one chooses to adopt and reject.

Similarly, Giddens's concept of routinization describes the ways routines, habits, and unconscious behaviors align people within and against specific social structures. These routine activities give life its sense of permanence and provide security in the face of change. Like Bourdieu, Giddens has attempted to create a theory that incorporates both agency and structure. Giddens calls this a theory of structuration, arguing that structures are essentially recursive in that they are both the outcome and the medium of human action. In other words, habits and routines are both the outcome of choices and a method for making choices.[4] For Giddens, such social systems are produced as "transactions" between agents. Social reproduction occurs as agents employ their knowledge of the rules of social systems and the resources available to them in specific contexts at different times.[5] I concluded chapter 3 by noting that in their discussions of structure and agency, both Bourdieu and Giddens emphasize social reproduction rather than social change. Because of this emphasis on reproduction, I argued that a more elaborate theory of structure, agency, and social change is still needed.

Chapter 4 further elaborated this discussion by examining the structural side of the agency:structure equation. By reviewing the work of Michel Foucault, I noted that although advocates of agency see structural work as too one-sided and deterministic, the pendulum can also sway too far the other way. By ignoring issues of structure, one misses recognizing the operations that give rise to systems and risks falling back into repressive structures.

Chapter 5, the story of Margaret's election campaign, examined the function of power within changing systems. The chapter began by discussing Foucault's notion of knowledge/power, which several writers argued was too deterministic and overwhelming to accurately portray the ways people use power in daily encounters. This theory was appended by Giddens's "reconstructed theory of power," which argues that power is created and reinforced when activities, routines, and belief systems are replicated in other times and places. While this argument seemed sufficient to explain the ways power operates within a social system, it could not explain how or why social systems change. At this point I contended that power can be seen more productively as the self-reflexive ability to control an image. This suggestion introduced the concept of image-power, which states that power resides in people's ability to control the ways in which they, and others, are perceived across social structures and times. Thus, a powerful organization is able to shape the identities of consumers, clients, and competitors in ways that are beneficial to itself. Powerful political candidates are able to shape how they are perceived by others and how others perceive their opposition. The concept of image-power reemphasizes the political nature of social change. It argues that issues of change and resistance should not be seen as natural or normal phenomena but rather as strategic movements of power, social interest, and control.

The current chapter builds on this theory of change by discussing the social level at which change is accessed. In other words, it will consider the study of change and look for the best ways to examine and record processes of change in social contexts. Here, we will return to the work of Bourdieu and his articulation of a theory of practice.

Identities and Cemeteries

One headstone is hard to miss when driving through Pleasant View Cemetery. The marker's black granite rises nearly five feet high and four feet wide, a monster surrounded by comparatively innocuous white and gray stones with names and dates engraved atop familiar Bible verses or sympathetic sayings: "will be missed," "life's work well done," "rest in peace."

MET AT OUR HIGH SCHOOL DANCE
MARRIED ON SAINT VALENTINE'S DAY 1944
WORKED LIFE TOGETHER
MARTHA THE ACCOUNTANT   GEORGE THE ENGINEER
ROMANCED THE WORLD TOGETHER
NOW IN THIS PLACE IN THE SUN AMONG RELATIVES AND FRIENDS
TOGETHER FOREVER

George and Martha's marker is noteworthy for more than just its imposing size. First, their lack of death dates indicate that neither

George nor Martha repose here. They are still living in town and pursuing their careers as an accountant and an engineer. Second, although most other markers identify people according to their familial roles—"beloved mother and wife," "devoted father," "baby," "son"—George and Martha have chosen to be immortalized according to their professional careers.

I'm not sure what to think about George and Martha's professional epitaph. On the one hand, they do not seem bothered that they will be immortalized by their careers, and the sheer size of their headstone offers much more insight into their life than the short phrases on the smaller stones around them. On the other hand, I wonder if George and Martha could be considered simple dupes of capitalism, willing to trade in their unique identities for professional brands and corporate titles. Many of my academic colleagues would think George and Martha successfully duped. Well, those who still subscribe to the notion of a coherent self would. Others would suggest that George and Martha's epitaph only deconstructs itself, meaning that in their attempt to immortalize a "self," they betray the notion of a self altogether. As such, George and Martha simply become a canvas on which institutions, governments, and other manifestations of late capitalism paint their own meanings. A distressing thought.

But, sitting on a bench on the Catholic side of Pleasant View Cemetery, I think about these academic accounts that argue that twentieth-century humanity has been reduced to complacent conformity within the shadow of the great corporation. As this story goes, we are nothing more than what our employers want us to be: submissive to authority, brand-loyal, suspicious of difference, culturally homogeneous, and too deep into debt to do anything about it. But as I look around at George and Martha's headstone, and at all the other engraved phrases jumping out at me, I wonder if it is too easy to view Microsoft, IBM, Time Warner, General Motors, or AT&T as endowed with forces much too powerful for simple individuals to resist. Besides, George and Martha identify themselves as more than just an engineer and an accountant. As I read their headstone, stories seem to fly out at me: two awkward high school students who meet in a corner of the gym at a school dance;

George the soldier and Martha his sweetheart, their families and friends assembled on Valentine's Day 1944, the day before George is sent back to Europe; George and Martha proudly starting a small business together; George and Martha about to travel on one of the first jet engine airplanes; George and Martha, "in this place in the sun among relatives and friends together forever."

In one sense, all of George and Martha's stories seem to be already written. All we need to do is place them in their respective roles as the main characters. In the same way that their headstone sits atop two empty, waiting graves, so too do untold stories wait for George and Martha to take them on, play them out, and record them into personal and cultural memories. No matter what George and Martha do between now and when they take their places here on the Catholic side of Pleasant View, there exists an already written story waiting to record and interpret their experience for them: George and Martha's retirement, George's midlife crisis, Martha's relationship with her mother, George's heart attack, Martha's life as a widow, and so on. No matter what happens, our culture provides George and Martha with unlimited stories to take on and use to interpret their life, understand what is happening to them, and position themselves within the culture around them.

This is not to say that George and Martha have no individual identity. In fact, the individual struggling for identity in the wake of faceless corporate power is one of our culture's most compelling stories. It is a story I see enacted here in front of me within Pleasant View Cemetery as each headstone proclaims an individual life against the multitude of structurally exact rows. But, it seems like our individuality emerges from the various ways in which we engage our stories and tailor them to fit our unique interpretations and plans. George might have a midlife crisis, but he might opt for vegetarian cuisine and bamboo rugs rather than a Silverado and a bass boat.

As I began working at Pleasant View, I encountered several lessons. The first emerged from my reflections on George and Martha and the stories they represent and enact. I soon learned that it is because of George and Martha's story, and the multitude of stories located here at Pleasant View, that the cemetery is so important as a cultural institution. The cemetery's identity and its value reside in its ability to tell stories both about the individuals memorialized here and about the general, collective, social grouping that occurs here. A cemetery is the ultimate storyteller, and it is the ultimate broker between structure and agency. I soon learned that this was why Andrew was so intent on keeping his cemetery out of the hands of Security Corp.

I consider Pleasant View Cemetery an organization, even though its inhabitants, who lived at various times over the past centuries, will never meet in an executive boardroom and are not busily developing strategic plans. A cemetery is an organization because it promotes specific values about human lives. It speaks to us about the very things we value: the importance of family genealogies, the existence and presentation of what we consider sacred, and the ways we want future generations to remember us. In his own writing about cemeteries, Foucault writes that the cemetery, which historically had a central place beside the church, has gradually been displaced to spaces outside of town. Here, in their displacement, cemeteries become an "other city." Cemeteries, like other privileged or sacred spaces set apart from society, constitute a heterotopia, an "othered space" that is removed from society but still essential to the ways society works.[6]

As an example of Foucault's "othered space," Pleasant View cemetery reveals many ways in which it is essential to my society. Its most prominent characteristic is the way it promotes and institutionalizes the cultural assumptions of those living in my city. In its structural design, the cemetery requires residents to align themselves with a major religious belief; it provides special recognition to those who have served in the armed forces, thus privileging the role the military plays within my community; and it rewards those individuals who have acquired large sums of wealth throughout their lives. In its various burial practices—ranging from the preparation and orientation of the body to the design and fabrication of the casket and the burial vault to the rituals performed at the interment—Pleasant View, like any other organization, reinforces, supports, and at times dictates a full spectrum of cultural values and social practices.

Researching Social Practice and Social Change

Where is the best place to study social change? What subjects lead to the most accurate descriptions of social change? How can we learn more about the process of change and its political, social, and economic consequences? Traditionally, social scientists and ethnographers have responded to such social questions by seeking the "objective relations" that form a society. These objective relations are defined as the formal rules that constitute a social group, hold that group together, and enable that group to function. Following this emphasis, researchers would visit and observe a social group, business, or other organization as an outsider and over time record the social rules that govern that group. Following anthropological terms, the resulting work is often considered a report on the "native experience" and a native representation of that experience. It is assumed that once the native experience of that group is recorded, questions concerning how change occurs, how people adapt to change, and what the implications of change are will emerge from the data.

Various writers have found this method problematic. Critics have argued that because such work emphasizes social order, it only records the experience of elite groups and social leaders. In many cases, this has led to an overrepresentation of some groups and an underrepresentation of others. It has also resulted in silencing or not representing voices of resistance or marginalized voices who do not fit with the dominant social paradigm of the group. As a result, rather than gaining a rich description of the social group, researchers only see what the elites want them to see. To an extent, these critiques raised problems of scope and inclusion rather than significant problems with research design or the ways in which research is conceptualized. But because of these critiques, many researchers have broadened their field of inquiry, listening to both the marginalized and the empowered as they attempt to build a more even picture of a social group.

Bourdieu has a more troubling critique of qualitative, ethnographic research. Bourdieu argues that a more serious issue in qualitative work is the researcher's relationship with the social system under investigation. Whereas most proponents of qualitative research emphasize the emotional distance, dispassionate observation, and neutral stance that is supposed to build an objective, disinterested accounting of social systems, Bourdieu argues that this relationship "contains the makings of a theoretical distortion." This distortion is created precisely because the researcher enters a community as an observer with no actual social role and no real place in the system under observation. The researcher has no function, no job, no direct method of interaction with people in the study group. And, more problematically, according to requirements of qualitative research design, not only does the researcher have no need to occupy a place in the system but also the researcher's disciplinary community would dissuade any active involvement within the research site.[7] Many suggest that becoming actively involved with the research group distorts the objectivity of the research and does not allow the researcher to have a complete, disinterested view.

However, Bourdieu argues that this objective, disinterested perspective creates a significant distortion in social analysis. He contends that what emerges from such research is not the everyday working knowledge of members of the social group but a distorted representation of this knowledge. Bourdieu calls the imposition of an observer's disinterested stance a "scholastic fallacy." What Bourdieu means is that a disinterested stance will impute to the research group interpretations and analyses that are more concerned with disciplinary academic questions than with practical issues of agents and their daily practices.[8] Researchers will study what they think is interesting rather than what members of the community under study think are important.

A second problem with the disinterested stance is that it is formed without "practical mastery" or competence in the research area. In other words, an academic expert in business communication can be someone who has observed, interviewed, and surveyed hundreds of business communicators but never practiced or developed a competence in the practical doing of business communication. In this case, the expert's questions, concerns, and interpretations will again deal more with issues that are interesting to other academics rather than practitioners of business communication. The result of this work is an academic's rendition of business communication in an organization and not a representation of the practical work business communicators do or the necessary day-to-day aspects of life within an organization.

Bourdieu argues that the knowledge gained by such observational research results in a "feel for the game" rather than a practical mastery of the game's skills.[9] Americans would call this the limited view of an "armchair quarterback," someone who has not actually played the game but has all the knowledge of an observer who can look back and rationally critique yesterday afternoon's game. Yet, as Bourdieu argues, this secondhand expertise has nothing in common with the impulsive, dynamic decisions made by the actual player in the middle of the game. He writes, "You need only think of the impulsive decision made by the tennis player who runs up to the net, to understand that it has nothing in common with the learned construction that the coach, after analysis, draws up in order to explain it and deduce communicable lessons from it."[10]

The conditions by which the coach can sit back and explain are not the same conditions in which the player must operate. For players, time is limited, information is not readily available, they are pressured to act, and they must act. Therefore, Bourdieu argues that the secondhand reports of objective observers are interpretations of practices, theories of theories, and not representations of experience. They are inaccurate misrepresentations, substitutes for actual practical mastery. Bourdieu notes that even the language of such objective analysis reveals its own outsiderness. Noting that representations of culture are often described as "maps," he notes that this "is the analogy which occurs to an outsider who has to find his way around a foreign landscape." The map allows the foreigner to compensate for his or her lack of practical mastery, something the native person takes for granted. This is why maps outline every possible alternative but do not indicate the best way to get from here to there.[11] Bourdieu notes that maps are the currency of outsiders in two ways. Most obviously, people who need maps are unfamiliar with the territory, and a map, even if constructed by a practical expert, will only outline sufficient information to achieve the outsider's goals. It will not include the subtleties known only to the native: shortcuts, landmarks, places to get gas, preferred restaurants, or radar traps. Second, maps occupy their own unique discursive space. In other words, maps are written according to their own specialized language requirements. We do not recognize a map's representation of terrain that is familiar to us—routes we might travel everyday, for example—until we take the time to properly align ourselves and interpret the map. Thus, the map is not the native's representation of his or her geography; it is a portrayal for outsiders of what they might see as they tour the native's terrain.

A Visit to Pleasant View

As I finish today's visit to Pleasant View, I marvel at the more than two thousand trees lining Pleasant View's roads, planted as a way to memorialize local soldiers who fought in World War I. Small plaques displaying soldiers' names, years of military service, and, if pertinent, the battles where they were killed are placed in front of the trees. The project continued into World War II and has continued since to memorialize soldiers who have fought in any war. I was surprised to see that many of these soldiers had not been just local citizens but had fought for and lived in countries that at one point were called enemies: Russia, Germany, Italy, and Japan.

In the evenings, Andrew and I would walk our dogs together along the river outside the city and talk about the cemetery, about the changes to the "death care" industry, and about the funeral directors' conference, where Andrew picked up several jokes, tales, and urban myths about life in the industry. "Real gallows humor," he said. He told me about the unpleasant, reclusive millionaire whose will specified that he be interred at 3:00 on a Saturday morning. Only four people attended the interment: the funeral director's assistant and a cemetery worker who were "appointed" by their supervisors, the millionaire's lawyer, and a homeless man who was sleeping in the cemetery. To everyone's surprise, after the interment, the lawyer informed the threesome that the deceased's will also specified that his multimillion dollar estate was to be divided equally among those who attended his burial. Another of Andrew's tales told of a woman who was a dedicated Nordstrom shopper. At her death, the entire local department store staff was invited to the funeral, where, atop her casket, someone had placed a golden

"Nordstrom box," which usually was used for customers' most elite purchases. When one store employee asked what the box was doing surrounded by flowers, cards, and other memorabilia, she was told that the woman's last request was to be cremated and then buried in a Nordstrom box.

Andrew told me that he likes his job, though he never intended to become the director of a cemetery. He has lived in this town his entire life, graduating five years ago from the local university with a bachelor's degree in commerce. At that time, he was working for the city as a self-appointed problem solver, computer expert, strategic thinker, and innovative planner. He was going to start an MBA but was offered the directorship at Pleasant View, a good opportunity to gain important managerial experience. He now admits, a year later, that he was not thinking about future promotional opportunities from the cemetery. Although he laughs when he says that he is in a "dead end" job, I can tell that there is some truth behind his joking.

The most difficult part of Andrew's job is assisting families whose children are killed in sudden accidents. Last summer, for example, a teenager was killed when his motorcycle collided with a Ford half-ton. His parents were still in shock when they walked into Andrew's office and ordered a $10,000 casket, an expensive headstone, prime cemetery location, and "all the fixings," as Andrew says. I could tell that Andrew had some misgivings with his career when he openly wondered if the family would have been better off donating the more than $20,000 to an accident prevention organization or a university scholarship program.

"Twenty thousand dollars," he said, "stuck in a hole. But, I guess it makes them feel better." Andrew shook his head when he told me that the young man's father kept saying that his son did not get to enjoy a full life, so he was not going to be denied anything in death. I was relieved that by then our dogs had found their way to the river and were anxiously waiting to chase the sticks we had gathered. It allowed me to change the subject.

It is now a brisk morning in October, several weeks after our walk in the park, and I am scheduled to meet Andrew in his office at Pleasant View. Each time I drive to the cemetery, I am struck by how difficult it is to get there. There is no direct road or intersection that leads to Pleasant View. I have to turn left off Twenty-third Street and then avoid driving into the front window of a Chinese restaurant by immediately turning right into a horizontal parking lot used by several monument dealers. I drive through the parking lot, dogleg to the left, and pass an old bakery, and suddenly I am in the cemetery. Andrew tells me that he is hoping that the city will buy the bakery "and either build a residence/office for the director, a crematorium, or both." Andrew enjoys the perversity of this, the bakery becoming a crematorium, which will become his official residence.

The cemetery office itself is small, a white rectangle with three steps and a steep wheelchair ramp up to the front doors. Immediately across the parking lot from the front doors is a huge map of the cemetery. The plastic containers for pamphlets and maps are empty. Once inside, the office looks like any other small business. There are two floors: the main floor, where two administrative assistants work behind a four-foot wall dividing the office space from the entranceway, and the basement, which holds the boardroom and Andrew's office. The carpet is brown shag, and once again I trip over the doormat that protects the carpet in winter.

I wait in one of the two chairs in the reception area as Andrew runs up the stairs from the basement. Pointing to his assistants, he says, "They're playing country music again! You'd think they could find something more cheerful." Leading me to the back of the administrative section, he gestures towards an open safe. "Here, take a look at these," he says as he pulls out an enormous accounting ledger veiled by a thick crust of dust. "Here is the history of the city," he explains as he opens the ledger. Inside, every burial at Pleasant View is listed by name, age, place of birth, date of death, price paid for the plot, and in some cases the cause of death and the person's occupation. The records resurrect a stunning view into early life in my city: John Clisby, the city's first police officer; Grace Fletcher, a leading area businesswoman; Edward William Meeres, aged twenty-seven, who, by wandering off in a prairie blizzard, became the city's first recorded death on January 14, 1888 (hypothermia). The records also provide a local history of disease and medicine at the creation of the city, a record of industrial and farming accidents, and the infant mortality rate in the early years of white settlement in the area.

Andrew next takes me for a drive through the cemetery itself. As we pass the stone pillars that distinguish the Catholic section from the Protestant, Andrew points out the area reserved for priests and nuns. We pass through the "nondenominational" area, for those who have not requested a specific section, and then through the section reserved specifically for infant deaths, their headstones displaying a lamb and simply reading "baby Alexander" or "baby Taylor." We then drive by the upright military section, where the thin, white headstones aligned in perfect rows contrast sharply with the flat military section, whose continuous grass carpet is broken only by a smooth hill rising in the center of the section. Pointing to the hill, Andrew says he is hoping to commission a monument for that spot next year, "maybe a jeep or a gun or something." Andrew then shows me the Ukrainian Orthodox section, each grave distinguished by a cross with two diagonal hashes across the vertical. We pass the Chinese and Greek sections, then stop at the university's section, where the Department of Anatomy inters those who have dedicated their bodies to science. There are only three granite headstones here; one reads "friend, sister, mother, baba, finally at peace." Surrounding the three are twenty-five other markers, small, round, flat circles with numbers etched on the top. Andrew explains that these are for "parts" that remain after the school is finished with the body.

As we continue through the cemetery, I see several stones with color photographs of the deceased, one with an artist's pallet engraved on the face of the stone, and another etched with a campsite, a recreational vehicle, and the words "the hours part us but they bring us back together again." I note that it has been nearly seven years since Mr. Fitchburg died. Mrs. Fitchburg's plot remains empty. I ask Andrew if there are any plots where wives or husbands obviously are not going to be reunited as they once hoped. "All kinds," Andrew says, then pointing to Mr. Fitchburg's grave adds, "but he doesn't know any better." Andrew's use of "he" reminds me of the "dark abodes" Foucault said every family has hidden within the cemetery. Another headstone displays a golf bag and nine iron.

As we drive along, Andrew shows me some of the more detailed headstones:

> NO ONE SAYS FAREWELL
> EVER REMEMBERED EVER LOVED
> SOLDIER OF POLAND
> PRAIRIE MAN
> BELOVED HUSBAND FATHER

He points out the Islamic section, where the graves are buried at a slight thirty-degree angle "so they are truer to an east-west axis," Andrew explains. "When they rise to meet Mohammed, they must be facing due east towards Mecca, and the cemetery isn't on a true north-south orientation, so we have to slightly angle the graves." Next, Andrew shows me the grave of a five-year-old boy who died in 1925. Andrew tells me that the boy had been accidentally backed over by a doctor's car; the doctor felt so bad that he had a life-sized statue made and placed on the boy's marker. However, today only the boy's shoes are left. "That statue has a history of its own," Andrew says; "it's been stolen, recovered, lost, found, and now no one knows where it is. But a local funeral home is building a bronze replica that we are going to put back on the broken marker."

On our way back to the office, Andrew points out two barely legible wooden markers from the early 1900s and a beautiful bronze engraving placed into a pink stone. The engraving reads:

> 1862–1921
> MOTHER WIFE AND MUCH LOVED FRIEND
> WITH WHAT SHE UNDERSTOOD OF THE MIND OF CHRIST
> SHE HEALED THE SICK AND BROUGHT COMFORT TO THE DESOLATE

As we complete our tour, Andrew tells me that he has a meeting downtown "with higher-ups," so I drop him off at his office. I drive out of the cemetery and back into the world.

Toward a Theory of Practice

In response to his critique of objective, disinterested social research, Bourdieu has articulated what he calls a theory of practice. Practice emphasizes an examination of life at a practical and a strategic level. In order to understand how individual agents operate in social groups, in workplaces, and in other interpersonal environments, researchers must look to practical, everyday knowledge and experience, and they must also experience decision making, risk taking, and relationship building within the social group they are studying. In theoretical terms, researchers must understand ways that distinguish material reality, social structures, and cultural structures and the ways these three components of social systems intersect with individual experiences and activities. Because an emphasis on practice relies equally on self-experience and theoretical analysis, a research agenda emphasizing practice attempts to overcome the long-standing opposition between theoretical knowledge and practical knowledge. Ideally, studies of practice should be designed to include both critically informed views of the everyday practices in which the researcher engaged and situated attempts to understand the social experience and strategies of the larger social group.

In attempting to overcome the divide between practical knowledge and theoretical knowledge, Bourdieu has tried to understand native experience in ways that validate that experience but do not simply take that experience at face value.[12] Additionally, Bourdieu argues that studies of practice must also, necessarily, be self-critical and self-reflexive. This self-reflexive component ensures that studies of practice do not fall into the same problems of objectivist reporting, which assumes that the researcher has no influence on the research site. Studies of practice acknowledge the influence of the researcher and expect that the researcher will become involved as an active participant in the research process. Like the tennis player who knows when to rush the net, the researcher should learn the practical behaviors, strategies, and consequences of life in the community while still retaining a critical perspective on these practices.

Bourdieu proposes an analysis focused on strategy and the strategies people use to function within social structures. Using again a metaphor from athletics, he suggests that a "good player is the game incarnate, [and] does at every moment what the game requires."[13] In the same way, social science researchers need to understand and examine the strategies involved in group behavior, in organizational cultures, and in the ways individuals negotiate the social structures around them.

Bourdieu has proposed three concepts that can help describe and examine social strategies: habitus, capital, and field. We have already examined the concept of habitus and have seen how it played a role in the ways people adapted and resisted to change at Access Bank. In discussing the concept of capital, Bourdieu is referring to the ways power is structured through a society. Thus, the state has tremendous capital in that it is able to exercise power at its will. Individuals may obtain capital through economic means as well as through social and cultural means. As noted in the previous chapter, Rex had greater cultural capital as a political candidate than Margaret, and she was unable to manufacture enough capital to offset Rex's position. But Bourdieu does not argue that capital works overtly. If capital was overt, if wealthy people received preferential treatment simply because they were wealthy, those without capital would be able to see that access to power is biased and arbitrary and not based on merit or democratic ideals. Such a system would "reveal the arbitrary character of the distribution of power and wealth."[14] Therefore, relations of capital must be symbolically mediated; they must be exchanged through symbols of capital rather than the use of capital itself. Therefore, certain symbols—manners, dress codes, automobile styles, addresses, vacation spots, language use, and pronunciation—stand in for the use of capital. Bourdieu refers to this as symbolic capital and proposes that researchers consider the ways in which groups use symbolic capital as social strategy: to differentiate themselves, select members, and wield power.

The concept of field traces the grounds on which habitus and capital operate. The field portrays an analysis of the relationships enacted by people as they take positions within and against the social groups around them. As Postone, LiPuma, and Calhoun write, "The position of a particular agent is the result of an interplay between that person's habitus and his or her place in a field of positions as defined by the distribution of appropriate forms of capital."[15] In this way, social analysis can better understand strategy by understanding how a person's intuited behavior (habitus) interrelates with the symbols of capital in play at a specific place at a specific time. Different fields exist, depending on the forms of capital and the goals of the community. Different fields can also meld into other fields. However, there are times when fields will resist incursions. For example, even though wealth may hold influence as capital in many fields, symbols of wealth may actually be resisted or scorned in other fields. Thus, fields are sites of struggles for power, legitimacy, intimacy, belonging, and activity. Fields are also sites of struggle as people attempt to define, change, or preserve them. For example, Pleasant View Cemetery can be seen as a field that different forces were struggling to define and change.

Rewriting Pleasant View Cemetery

After watching me spend over a month reading, listening, and wandering at Pleasant View, Andrew began asking about the business plan. The city council was to vote on Security Corp.'s offer in a few months, and without the plan, there would be little to compete with against such a compelling bid. I, on the other hand, was wondering why so many people (myself included) resist cemeteries and rarely think about them and how the city council could forget that they owned and managed Pleasant View. I realized that Andrew and I needed to change several key aspects of Pleasant View, but I had difficulty knowing where to start.

Ironically, one of the biggest problems with Pleasant View was that it was basically successful, but one could not tell this because the cemetery displayed no symbolic capital. It continued on, year after year, meeting its budget, maintaining its facilities, repairing occasional vandalism, never becoming problem enough to warrant any scrutiny or interest.

Pleasant View's success was not just limited to its finances. As I mentioned before, I began to see Pleasant View as an organization because it promotes specific values about human lives. It preserves and promotes what we consider important and worth remembering. After some time at Pleasant View, I began to see that this function of the cemetery had become taken for granted, and no one would mention it. In the same way that the city's elected politicians did not even know that the city owned and operated Pleasant View, most of the people who worked there had little interest or awareness of the cultural work the cemetery did. In fact, the cemetery's cultural work seemed to be forgotten. It was certainly poorly defined, and in all my initial conversations at Pleasant View, I was told that the cemetery existed simply "to bury people." Pleasant View was successful at promoting a cultural story most people had forgotten. In addition, the cemetery had no way to show its cultural success because it had no way to communicate its symbolic capital. We needed to change the cemetery's habitus into its symbolic capital.

In other words, Pleasant View was so successful at promoting and advancing its organizational objectives (and the resulting political and social assumptions that these sustained) that these objectives had been naturalized and made part of our community's unconscious: people are buried according to their religious affiliation; they are buried in family plots, in expensive wood caskets, surrounded by a concrete vault; headstones announce the deceased's place within the nuclear family. The cemetery's "perpetual care fund" provides eternal maintenance for each grave, and flowers are placed on graves each spring. We needed to de-naturalize these assumptions and show people the vital role Pleasant View played in maintaining and recording this community's religious, social, economic, and cultural capital.

In talking to Andrew about this problem, I borrowed the term "repressed" to describe Pleasant View's culture. It was there, it was effective, but few people ever noticed or identified it—it was repressed. But since Pleasant View's cultural work was repressed, city leaders could perceive the cemetery only in the ways that Security Corp. projected. It was as if Pleasant View's image was being presented as a reflection in a mirror designed by Security Corp. Thus, the cemetery became defined according to Security Corp.'s financial discourse, and city politicians fell in line with this financial discussion, asking only about the financial status of the cemetery: Does it break even? Does it make money? Is it worth $2 million? No other factors were part of this discussion. The very fact that Pleasant View's business plan would become the strategic report upon which its fate rested demonstrated the extent to which Security Corp. was in control of this story, and as a necessary corollary, this contest.

Previous chapters have discussed the roles narratives and images play in organizations and social groups. What I saw happening at Pleasant View was a discordance between these two components of organizational identity. Pleasant View's narratives presented one story about the cemetery, while its image presented quite a different one. Apart from its accounting ledger, Pleasant View did not regularly prepare any organizational writing. The cemetery had never prepared a business plan, it had no strategic planning documents, nor did it have any written history or comprehensive log about the day-to-day operations there. In more technical terms, one can call this lack of systematic, strategic, or even historical writing the lack of an organizational discourse, which meant that the cemetery had no way to influence its external image. Although it had a compelling (if repressed) internal narrative, its lack of any significant organizational communication meant that there were no real ways for this narrative to influence the cemetery's larger image. Thus, Pleasant View was an organization with what Stuart Culver has called a distressed discourse, a discourse that is incapable of sustaining the larger identity of an organization.[16]

It would be very easy to come away from this finding and hunt through Pleasant View, looking for the "central discourse" that would structure all of the business relations within the organization. However, my encounters with Pleasant View showed me the extent to which the cemetery is an amalgamation of religious, ethnic, financial, geographical, and bureaucratic discourses. In turn, these discourses are comprised of hundreds of individual voices, each with their own distinct story: the five-year-old boy whose bronze statue will soon fill his empty shoes; the soldier who, arriving two days late, is distinguished to be the only member of Custer's Seventh Cavalry to have survived the Little Big Horn; the local boy "who lost his life when The Landovery Castle was sunk by the Germans June 27, 1918."

Rationally, I realized that very little exists under the granite headstone marked "Grace Fletcher"; yet I still see in that headstone a symbol that unleashes the story of my city's first women's advocate, someone who was instrumental in extending the franchise to women and in guaranteeing legal protection for women in the new settlement that eventually became my city. The numerous voices from the past and present that make up Pleasant View Cemetery— voices like Grace Fletcher's—are imaginary, historic, compelling, but repressed. As such, Pleasant View's symbols required a sustained organizational discourse to evoke the voices, stories, and memories that resided here.

These imaginary voices, however, can only be accessed and activated through language. Without the intervention of speech or writing, these markers remain dormant and their discourse remains inaccessible. Thus, the writing and the speech produced within organizations achieve more than a simple communicative function; they evoke the organization's stories, create the organization's culture, and build the organization's identity. Since most of the writing produced by Pleasant View was numerical and statistical and Security Corp.'s writing was financially driven and defined according to its profits and market size, Pleasant View's identity, its worth and its value, was constructed according to Security's story: solely according to numbers, financial bottom lines, and potential selling prices.

I recommended to Andrew that Pleasant View develop alternative ways to evoke its unique organizational stories. Theoretically, my goal was to use this new organizational discourse to re-align Pleasant View's discordant organizational identity. These stories were presented both in our business plan and in alternative genres that promoted the cemetery as a vibrant cultural institution. Though I was retained by Pleasant View to write a business plan, I found myself in the end writing a collection of organizational stories. Certainly, traditional models of business plans do not usually designate a section for "corporate narratives," but I used my symbolic capital as an "expert" in business communication to write one anyway. After the necessary summaries and table of contents, the business plan I prepared for Pleasant View opened with a ten-page history, complete with color pictures, structured in a question-and-answer format. Titled "Preserving Our Past—Planning Our Future," this opening section of the business plan narrated and thereby constructed Pleasant View's identity as a valuable city institution. It told many of the stories repeated in this chapter and connected these stories to the larger cultural identity of my city.

After the introductory narrative, Andrew and I decided to divide the business plan into two further sections, an informational guide and an operations management guide. The informational guide outlined the role Pleasant View plays within the city and the surrounding region, explained the city's role within the local "death care" industry, and presented the various services Pleasant View offers local citizens as well as individuals and groups who visit Pleasant View from around the world. In fact, very few locals were aware that people often came from far away to visit several famous historic graves located at Pleasant View. One of these sites included the grave of an international Buddhist priest who died when visiting the city for a religious conference. To use Bourdieu's terms, this section, along with the plan's opening narrative, built the cultural capital of the cemetery. It strategically pointed to the religious, business, political, and social leaders who were buried in the cemetery. Then, it used this capital to argue that current city leaders could not disown the responsibility entrusted to them by previous generations.

In contrast to the informational guide, the operations guide provided a financial blueprint for future operations, building the economic capital in the report. This section predicted expenditures and revenues for the next five years and anticipated new trends and industry directions. This is also where Andrew placed his wish list: a crematorium and a new section for cremations, an indoor chapel and visitors' site, and a floral shop on the cemetery grounds (profits going to the perpetual care fund).

In addition to the business plan, Andrew and I developed other ways for Pleasant View to voice its stories and thereby reconcile its image and its narrative. Andrew commissioned a local student to design a web page that would profile individual stories of those reposing at Pleasant View. This "virtual cemetery" will eventually enable people buried at Pleasant View to be represented by their own material (pictures, video, prose) on the cemetery's web site. Using electronic headstones, visitors will be able to click on linked images and scroll through the many stories that Pleasant View holds. We also planned to expand the cemetery's walking tours and advertise the cemetery as an excellent location for running, bicycling, and roller-blading, and we initiated a public information campaign designed to teach the local community about Pleasant View and the many stories it holds.

These projects were all based on the conclusion that Pleasant View was not able to control its external image. Because it had lost control of this image, the cemetery was unknown by the community, and other agents in the market were creating the cemetery's image. As a result, the cemetery's social desirability, the value of its service to my community, and its economic value were being structured entirely by external forces. In addition, as its image was further distanced from its narratives, as other agents began to define its image, Pleasant View began losing its power. However, once Pleasant View regained the ability to write/speak its narrative and project this narrative through its business plan, a proposed marketing and information campaign, its new "virtual cemetery," and other new projects it has started, it became able to influence and recreate its external image. It was able to assert its role within the community and recognize its unique cultural and historical position. By re-aligning its narrative and its image and by regaining control over its external image, the cemetery also regained its power.

By remaining in control of its organizational discourse, Pleasant View was also better able to control its identity by recreating its image of itself. A organization that is able to control its narrative and its image, and ensure that these two components of its identity are mutually supporting, is better able to position itself within the marketplace and present a unique identity to its customers. In addition, a strong identity helps employees better identify with their company, it teaches the history of the company along with its goals and objectives, and it helps to create roles and role models for new employees. Although Pleasant View had a narrative, its story was limited to perhaps half a dozen people. By reinventing and broadcasting a new corporate story, we were able to recreate Pleasant View as a vital public institution. As we wrote in the business plan:

[Our city] believes that cemeteries are important spiritual, historical, aesthetic, and civic spaces that continue to serve present, future, and past residents of our community and our world. Pleasant View Cemetery provides residents a place apart from daily activities to memorialize and show respect for loved ones in a dignified, peaceful, and quiet setting. City residents make considerable daily use of Pleasant View, visiting graves, walking, jogging, and bicycle riding through the parks, and by exploring the history preserved here. In addition, people from throughout the world have traveled to Pleasant View to conduct genealogical research, visit specific graves, or to purchase, visit, or admire one of the more than 2000 trees lining Pleasant View that are dedicated to people from around the world who have served in their country's Armed Forces.

Our goal in writing the business plan was to promote the cemetery's symbolic capital and, in doing so, change Pleasant View into a priceless civic institution. We believed that even though the cemetery was financially self-sufficient and did not cost the city any money to operate, the possibility of an instant cash infusion of $2 million would easily overwhelm any financial argument we could make. In fact, Security Corp. had used that argument to win over many other cemeteries in many other towns like mine. We needed to create a different story with a different conclusion, and by developing a new story for Pleasant View, we successfully challenged and defeated Security Corp.'s proposal. Andrew was given permission to expand and develop the cemetery's products and services, and he gained considerable recognition for his proactive business plan.

Who wrote this story of change, and what did the story hope to accomplish? Working together, Andrew and I wrote the business plan as an attempt to defeat Security Corp.'s proposed buy-out of the cemetery. From our perspective, our community benefited from this story and from the way we resurrected the stories that lay hidden at Pleasant View. I am sure Security Corp. would disagree with this conclusion, and they may even argue that our work will ultimately hurt our city's cemetery and our community. However, practice-based research is about action, about choices, and about consequences. I could have remained disinterested in Andrew's fate and simply watched, recorded, and then wrote about the cemetery's demise or success. I could have interviewed executives from Security Corp. and from the city government to create a more balanced report. And, once it was all over, I could have theorized why Security Corp. was successful and argued that their takeover of the cemetery is another example of the globalization of capital and the need for local resistance and activism. But, who would have benefited from this disinterested perspective? Security Corp. might have. Perhaps the cemetery might have benefited, as it became en-folded into a wealthy North American conglomerate. In addition, perhaps my academic discipline would have preferred a disinter-ested report, since the knowledge that such a report would gener-ate would be more suited to the questions, theories, and perspec-tives of other academics.

At the same time, knowing about Pleasant View and knowing that other people in my community were sympathetic to our joint ownership of this institution, I do not regret taking action and be-coming involved in what I thought was a necessary cause. What are the consequences of this story? Pleasant View Cemetery will remain city-owned, Security Corp. will not be able to gain a foothold in this community, and Andrew will keep his job. In addition, this story tells about a successful and meaningful academic/community partnership. It suggests that academics can play a positive role in their communities and presents a model for research practices that does not simply ignore social consequences. At the same time, these consequences are selective and admittedly biased. In the end, the success of this model and this story really depends on kinds of re-search, community activism, and community partnerships it inspires.

Since my encounter with Andrew and Pleasant View Cemetery, I make it a habit to visit old, abandoned cemeteries. On a recent trip through Montana, Idaho, and Utah, Rebecca and I discovered a pioneer settlement cemetery in rural Utah. Here we visited fifteen pioneer graves, each surrounded by picket fences and obscured by seventy-five years of sagebrush and evergreens. In central Utah we found the graves of twenty immigrants who in the mid-1800s had left Sweden to eventually settle in the middle of a desert. In Montana's hills we found the grave of a pioneer woman who was born in the mid-1800s in Halifax, Nova Scotia. We stopped at a roadside cemetery in Idaho that sorrowfully detailed a nineteenth-century family's struggle to tame the West. Four children shared the same date of death, and their mother's plot was filled shortly there-after. Now, rather than quickly pass a cemetery by, I try to stop and visit. I pull grass away from its headstones, straighten and replant its plastic flowers, read its inscriptions, and imagine—and relive—its stories.

7 ■ ORGANIZATIONAL CHANGE AS COMMUNITY ACTION

> It was an extravagant winter, with new records set for both snow and all-time low temperatures. My father seemed to be always outside shoveling snow in the dark, piling up huge icy banks all around the house. He would come in from the cold red-cheeked and handsome, trying to put his icy hands around my neck.
>
> —Diane Schoemperlen, *Hockey Night in Canada*

> "But isn't everything here green?" asked Dorothy.
> "No more than any other city," replied Oz; "but when you wear green spectacles, why of course everything you see looks green to you."
>
> —L. Frank Baum, *The Wonderful Wizard of Oz*

Snow Shovels and Identity Stories

My high school calculus class was as much about mathematics as it was about Gordie Howe. Our teacher—tall, slate-haired, and impeccably dressed—was passionate about three things: derivatives, volleyball, and hockey. Don, as we called him, would regularly stop in midequation to diagram a new volleyball strategy for attacking a weak back court or to sketch a clever way to isolate a player at the top of the blue line for a quick slap shot. The complexities of calculus sparked in Don's mind a kaleidoscope of patterns, interweaving plays, and differentiating figures. For him, there was little difference between two trains leaving opposing stations and a puck hurled towards an open top corner. In his mind, the x's and o's of jock talk effortlessly intermingled with definite integrals, partial fractions, and converging series.

Don's hero was Gordie Howe. Throughout that winter term, whenever he sensed that our energy was ebbing, burdened with midsemester fatigue, he'd remove his ever-present blue jacket, loosen his burgundy tie, roll up his sleeves, and tell us about Gordie Howe. Don's eyes would turn a brighter hue as he described play after play, goal upon goal, while my scant mathematical aptitude would give way to the wake of Mr. Hockey. Born in Floral Saskatchewan, Howe played center, right wing, and defense; won six Hart Trophies; was named to the NHL's first all-star team twelve times; participated in four Stanley Cup victories; made 1,071 career goals and 1,518 career assists; and had twenty-seven consecutive seasons in which he scored twenty or more goals. The numbers kept coming, and we didn't mind if they had little to do with that day's assignment.

"Do you know how Gordie Howe got so strong?" was the way Don would start his favorite Gordie Howe story. "Snow shoveling!" Don would then tell us how, in one of his interviews, Howe spoke of his hours of snow shoveling and how the repetitive lifting and throwing of season after season of the prairie's dry weight built his arms into tree limbs. For years, each winter morning, Don's story was equally motivating and antagonizing as I staggered out of bed to clear driveways. Ever since I was old enough to want a hockey stick, I've shoveled driveways. And though my morning gigs were lucrative, a good weekend could be downright excessive. A good Friday night snowfall multiplied by six to eight driveways could net ski and boot rental, a lift ticket, two cheeseburgers, poutine (french fries, gravy, and melted cheese), and a hot chocolate.

Moving from home to college put an end to my small business and my hope for Gordie Howe–inspired forearms. But, when Rebecca and I moved from Utah to our own first house in northwestern Canada, I was thrilled to have my very own driveway. I bought a snow shovel in October and waited for winter's first snowfall. This being Gordie Howe's home province, I didn't have to wait long. By Halloween, small icy piles were growing along the driveway's edges as the snow kept falling.

We had moved into an older neighborhood; of the twelve homes on our block, ten housed senior citizens. Our immediate neighbor,

Hermina, was nearly eighty-five years old and pencil thin, certainly past her snow shoveling prime. So, I volunteered to clear her driveway and sidewalks when I cleared mine. I had a good system going. I would shovel my way out of our driveway, clean the sidewalk to Hermina's, shovel my way up her driveway until I reached her back door, then shovel my way back down to the sidewalk. I diligently kept up my route morning after morning until one particularly snowy morning when Hermina's friend across the street called. Helen Wolouski wanted to know if I would shovel her driveway too. Four months ago, her husband Donald had undergone a triple bypass operation after his second heart attack. She thought that another winter of shoveling snow would probably kill him.

I completed my loop around Hermina's place and then walked over to Helen and Donald's home. The snow had drifted against their garage, and the pile was a good five feet high. For the next twenty minutes I was busy removing the snow mound, layer by layer. Soon I had found my rhythm and was making steady progress when I was interrupted by a muffled voice shouting at me from the back door.

"What the hell are you doing?" the voice demanded. I stopped, straining to hear over my breathing. I removed my tuque so I could hear better. "What the hell are you doing?" it demanded again. Coming out of the back door was Mr. Wolouski, dressed head to foot in winter work gear, looking a little like Harry Morgan's Colonel Potter on a bad day in Siberia.

"Hi," I started, "I'm cleaning your driveway."

"Well, yes, I can see that," growled Mr. Wolouski. "Why?" His question was absorbed by the falling snow, and we stood there together in icy white silence for a few moments. My ears were starting to hurt from the cold; my eyelashes had frozen together long ago.

"Because your wife—" I began, but I never finished the sentence.

"My wife? My wife's got some damn fine ideas." Helen had obviously neglected to tell Donald that the new guy from across the street was going to shovel *his* driveway. "Well, you shouldn't listen to my wife," he said abruptly. "Now get on home and mind your own business."

He was angry and serious, so I took my shovel and retreated to the sanctity of my own driveway. About an hour later, my phone rang. It was Helen. "Sorry Donald was so rough on you today," she commented. I didn't know if I should be angry or worried, so I simply asked her if she had told him I would be coming over to help out. "Oh, of course not," she said, startled, "he would never let you get started. Donald is very independent that way. But you will help out again, next snowfall." This was not so much a question as a statement. She hung up.

The next major snowfall brought with it a dilemma. Up to this point, Helen, Donald, and I had an effective truce. Not enough snow had accumulated to spark any movements on either side of the snow-packed neutral zone. However, this being January in northern Saskatchewan, the inevitable soon came. It started with a small flurry Thursday morning, and by midafternoon the schools had closed, buses were slowing down service, and the locals were stocking four-day provisions. By six o'clock, grocery stores had run out of pierogies and the video store's new releases shelf was empty. By midnight, the wind had begun to sweep the snow into long powdery ridges and rippling waves of surf. The next morning we woke up to a silent, frozen ocean outside our window. The driveway, sidewalk, and front lawn were obscured by a single layer of unbroken snow. My piles of neatly stacked snow-shoveling residue, remnants of battles past, were buried by the new drifts: waves suddenly frozen seconds before crashing into a nonexistent reef.

It took me twenty minutes to carve a trail out my driveway. An hour later I had successfully breached Hermina's front walk. As I began pitching snow off Hermina's front porch, I saw Mr. Wolouski struggle out of his garage with a gasoline-powered snowblower. I sensed the inevitability of the moment. Mr. Wolouski fired up the machine and began to ponderously attack the wall of snow drifting across his driveway. He was not strong enough to control the machine's lurching and skidding wheels and its torquey, aggressive blades. Without saying anything, I waded over and began pitching snow into the turning blades of the snowblower. We meticulously worked our way across the driveway, me gathering snow and pitching it into the waiting blades of the snowblower. We never spoke, he never looked at me, and the machine pulsed on, spewing snow into silent mountains and dense ridges. Once we finished, I waded back across the neutral zone to finish Hermina's sidewalk.

We continued this way, me throwing piles of snow into Mr. Wolouski's churning machine, for three more months of snowfalls and a few more day-long blizzards. It was hard for Mr. Wolouski. As I watched him quiver around the driveway clutching the snowblower's trigger, I could imagine him, years ago, as a young boy crawling out of bed at sunrise to shovel other people's driveways. He was building Gordie Howe forearms, helping the older people in his neighborhood, making some money for skiing. Now, that story had caught up to him, like the great gunfighter in a John Ford western who realizes, too late of course, that thirty years of farming hasn't made him any quicker on the draw, or Rock Hudson, playing the weathered oil tycoon opposite James Dean in *Giant*, who gets beat up by a couple of punks in a roadside bar. Mr. Wolouski was fighting change.

I was not helping Mr. Wolouski's battle. In fact, I was too busy trying to enact my own self-absorbed stories of agency, philanthropy, and identity to recognize or even understand the ways Mr. Wolouski was struggling to retain some semblance of his own identity and agency. My world was making perfect sense. I was building a new home, shoveling snow, developing my arms, contributing to my community, helping out my neighbors. I was the embodiment of Lord Baden Powell's mission. But Mr. Wolouski's world was falling apart, and my actions played into the dynamic of stories and interpretations closing in on him: the stories his wife was creating, telling him he was too old to complete tasks around the house; the stories he was telling himself about his operation, his recovery, and his autonomy; and the stories the neighbors were telling about this proud army veteran who could no longer clear his own driveway.

To his credit, Mr. Wolouski and I eventually became judicious friends. I found out that he worked Thursday and Friday evenings as a security guard at the local library. I would often drop by to read car magazines, and he would tell me about his days as a combat soldier in World War II and his life since the war. I was impressed by the pride he took in his job. His security uniform was always pressed, his hat clean and straight, his white collar stiff from extra starch, his black shoes polished. He told me about the time our neighborhood was a wheat field, how his was the first house in the area, and how he watched my house being built. "Good solid house," he would say. His stories would always last until a few minutes past the library's closing, providing him the pleasure of kicking me out and the right to scold me for keeping him from his closing duties.

The stories Mr. Wolouski told himself, his family, the patrons at the library, and his neighbors were strategic stories, told to persuade, to generate action, to incite resistance, to gain and deflect power. But more importantly, these were stories about identity. Put into the context of organizations, identity-stories provide agents within organizations ways to define themselves within and against cultural, historical, social, organizational, and economic structures. Identity-stories are powerful because they interpret perceptions of everyday life. They become filters through which people interact with the world. In some cases, identity-stories are useful. They act as protective counterweights to a daily barrage of messages, constructions, and images. A strong organizational narrative will protect an organization and help it deal with the competing stories around it. At the same time, identity-stories can be dangerous because, as filters, they can limit a field of vision and establish a false sense of security that distracts from important matters at hand. An organization can be so focused on its own identity-story that it ignores the identity-stories competitors, clients, suppliers, and customers are telling.

As I have argued in this book, identity is constructed in the intersection of narratives and images. Narratives are the internal stories people within organizations tell themselves; images are the external accounts of how others perceive the organization. When narratives and images clash, when they no longer support each other, an organization's identity becomes conflicted and problematic. This conflict can have significant implications for organizational leadership, strategic vision, employee morale, company ethics, and ultimately the survival of the organization. An organization that loses its identity has no motivating structure and no reason to stay in business.

An organization without an identity is also an organization without a discourse. In such cases, people within the organization need to re-articulate the organization's narratives and rebuild its images. What is most interesting, most vital, and yet still most misunderstood about this process of change is that in order for it to be successful, it must transgress existing communicative patterns, styles, and formats. Academics call repetitive and typical communication styles and patterns "genres," and in recent years, genre scholars have documented the ways an organization's writing (and other forms of communication) is often contained by dominant power structures within an organization. What this means is that power is embedded not only within what an organization says but also in how it says it, the processes that go into the formation and release of corporate texts. As a result, an organization cannot change if it maintains its existing communication processes, styles, forms, and procedures.

However, this is only half the picture. As the cases in this book have shown, when people transgress genres, violate boundaries, and intentionally break with routine practices, change becomes a possibility. Of course, as the case of MacKenzie College and Margaret's nomination campaign showed, such practices will also generate opposition by those people whose interests are threatened by change. However, as was seen at the massage school and Pleasant View Cemetery, communication can occur in nongeneric forms. It can be ad hoc, temporary, disposable, and transitory. In these cases, communication—and writing specifically—seems to be more strategic than genre-based since it is willing to manipulate and even violate genres in order to spark change.

Pushing this point, one could argue that too much emphasis on organizational genres at the expense of more temporal and fleeting forms of communication may tend to re-assert and support the status quo in organizational contexts. In order to be studied, genres must be able to be replicated over time and place. This condition requires stable work environments, uniform practices, and a lack of change. Alternatively, more strategic studies, those studies that examine temporal and ad hoc writing in the contexts of change, bring a richer, more dynamic, and more controversial political focus with them.

As I noted in chapter 1, following Herndl and Nahrwold's work, the decision to study prevailing genres or the decision to study change is as much a political decision as it is an academic one. The communicative dynamics of change—the fleeting temporal statements, the attempts to transgress genres, and the writings that violate boundaries—will be noticed only by the researcher who learns through practice. Simply observing a context will not provide enough practical insight to see nongeneric practices. As the previous chapter argued, this "feel for the game" can only come from experience. If one approaches workplace research from the perspective of an outsider who will create a "map" of a workplace's communication, one will not witness or recognize more fleeting, nongeneric communication patterns. These are only accessible to the person who has an insider's working knowledge of the organization. Thus, to understand genre, one approaches an organization as an outsider who will observe and record repetitive, stable practices. To understand change, one must participate, experience, and become involved in actual acts of change. Each position carries with it separate but real political consequences for the research and the researcher.

About two years after I took on the position of an academic consultant, I accepted a position as an assistant professor at Clarkson University in Potsdam, New York. Although I left northern Canada, Mr. Wolouski, the world of Canadian politics, my cemetery, and my consultancy, I have continued to remain involved in the world of nonprofit organizations, community development, and action research. However, this has not been a simple transformation. As Bourdieu has noted, the world of the university and of academic disciplines is not the world of entrepreneurial consulting, nor is it the world of community advocacy, nonprofit organizations, and political campaigns.

Other researchers have also noted the differences between what is called academic writing and professional or workplace writing. Patrick Dias, Aviva Freedman, Peter Medway, and Anthony Paré have stated that these forms of writing are "worlds apart." They argue that "writing at work and writing in school constitute two very different activities" because one type of writing is concerned with schooling while the other is oriented towards "accomplishing the work of an organization."[1] These authors raise an important point, noting that at school, students do not need to produce arguments or text for which they will be held accountable in any real way. Student writing rarely serves any purpose other than showing what one has learned, and the issue of getting a high grade is very different from issues of legal liability, public safety, or salvaging a damaged company. As such, most classroom writing has no real stake in anything. Student projects are rarely produced to encourage action, take leadership, or solve a problem. As a consequence, few universities are actually enabling student writers for the world of work.

While some academics may not find this problematic, others find real problems with a system of higher education that graduates adults who cannot effectively communicate outside of a classroom setting. But the argument is not quite that simple. Dias, Freedman, Medway, and Paré not only claim that these are two very different kinds of writing but also that, because writing is so context-dependent, it is nearly impossible to cross between (transcend) worlds of work and worlds of school. A teacher cannot simply translate between work and school and hope that students will recognize and remember their rhetorical lessons when they reach the workplace.[2]

At the same time, these authors miss an important point. Like workplace writing, student writing also "accomplish[es] the work of an organization." But in this case, that organization is the university. Here, writing is not fully the problem. In contexts of work and contexts of school, people are learning how to use writing to fulfill the work of their unique organizations. The real problem is that the work of the university has very little to do with the work of the rest of the world. As a result, the work of the university isolates students from experiences that have meaning outside of the university. The written products that are produced within and for the university perpetuate this problem.

Shortly before I moved to northern New York, I overheard a conversation between a retired farmer and a university admissions official at a large, publicly funded university. Dressed in green overalls and a plaid shirt, the farmer stood out in the lineup of eighteen and nineteen year olds in baggy pants and knapsacks. The admissions official greeted the gentleman by saying that the school could not release student records to relatives without the student's permission. The man was taken aback: he was not looking for student records; he wanted to sign up for courses. He had filled out his enrollment information, selected his courses, and was ready to pay his tuition up front—in cash.

The admissions officer was bewildered. She had never encountered this situation before. She called her manager, who politely asked the man if he had a high school transcript. The man said he had finished high school in the 1940s and his one-room schoolhouse had been bulldozed in the 1960s. He didn't know where his transcript was. The manager insisted that he needed this high school transcript to apply to the university. The farmer politely asked what relevance a 1940s high school transcript would have today. He then explained to the manager that for the past forty-five years, his taxes had supported a university he had never attended. He had recently retired, he had sold his farm, he had plenty of time and money, and now he wanted in.

The farmer presented a good case. After supporting this institution for nearly half a century, why should he not be able to take a few courses, for interest, during his retirement? And yet, a university system based on credentials, academic records, and preparing young people for jobs was unable to help him. This university did not have a discourse, a language, that included him. In the end, he left, disappointed, but promising to try again.

Like my neighbor Mr. Wolouski, many North American universities have been telling themselves an identity-story that is no longer credible. To use the terminology of this book, the university's narratives are no longer supported by its image. As a result, there is a significant discordance in the ways those within higher education view the university and the ways outside groups view this same institution. Weakened by fiscal cutbacks, ideological debates, downsizings, and a de-professionalizing economy and job market, the university's identity has recently become vulnerable to the image-power of governments, corporations, interest groups, philanthropic organizations and foundations, and even tax-paying retirees.

Reading and Writing Change in Higher Education

This issue returns us to some of the original questions and the initial context that introduced this book. As I have argued previously, and as was shown in the story of MacKenzie College, higher education is facing difficult challenges to its educational, research, and social missions. At the same time, many of our communities are facing significant challenges as well. As more and more of our energies and ambitions are directed by global interests, worldwide electronic networks, and multinational business ventures, citizens seem to be distancing themselves from local community interests, from neighborhoods and public spaces, and from community-building initiatives. Our communities are facing problems in race relations, poverty, decaying infrastructures, weakening citizen participation and input, and a lack of strong civic leadership. Robert Putnum has shown that over the past decade, there has been a consistent decline in rates of political and community participation in America. Since the 1960s, Americans' memberships in associations, parent-teacher organizations, and other civic clubs and organizations have also declined. These rates, coupled with declining religious participation, union membership, and other forms of community participation, suggest that we have become increasingly disconnected from the people around us and the power structures that influence our lives.[3] This retreat from local spaces has already been noted by several social researchers and community workers who have warned that as our community connections decay and deteriorate, we are losing the important social connections people rely on in times of family stress, economic downturns, employment problems, health crises, and other social problems.[4]

In a 2000 report on leadership, written for the W. K. Kellogg Foundation, Alexander Astin and Helen Astin raise many of these same concerns. For Astin and Astin, this problem has its roots in a lack of leaders emerging from today's university system. They argue that there is "mounting evidence that the quality of leadership in this country has been eroding in recent years." Defining leadership as both elected and appointed officials and the work done by individual citizens, they note that "too few of our citizens are actively engaged in efforts to effect positive social change."[5] Further, Astin and Astin claim that this lack of citizen input in civic and community life can be traced to a lack of leadership education and leadership role modeling in universities. The report argues:

> Students will find it difficult to lead until they have experienced effective leadership as part of their education. They are not likely to commit to making changes in society unless the institutions in which they have been trained display a similar commitment. If the next generation of citizen leaders is to be engaged and committed to leading for the common good, then the institutions which nurture them must be engaged in the work of the society and the community, modeling effective leadership and problem solving skills, demonstrating how to accomplish change for the common good. This requires institutions of higher learning to set their own house in order, if they expect to produce students who will improve society.[6]

Arguing that leadership "is a process that is ultimately concerned with change," Astin and Astin state that universities have not given enough attention to the concept of leadership and civic responsibility in the classroom and in the way university professionals go about their own business.[7] They argue for greater emphasis on learning personal qualities that will foster capable leaders: "self-understanding, listening skills, empathy, honesty, integrity, and the ability to work collaboratively." In addition, Astin and Astin claim that students are influenced equally by what universities do as by what they say, suggesting that the way academics govern themselves, how they model professional lives, and how they run their universities will also influence the values students gain at institutions of higher education.[8]

In an address to the 2000 Council for Advancement and Support of Education (CASE) Conference on Corporate and Foundation Fundraising, Scott Cowen, president of Tulane University, raised many similar concerns about the issues facing both our universities and our communities.[9] Cowen noted that a changing higher education environment is placing new demands and expectations on universities. For the first time in their history, there is an increased emphasis on accountability within universities as they are being asked to report and justify retention rates, graduation rates, job placements, and the kinds of learning students achieve. People who financially support universities through tuition, donations, taxes, or research grants want to know how this money is used and what kind of results are achieved with their support.

Cowen also noted an increasing amount of competition in the field of higher education as corporations, for-profit universities, trade schools, virtual electronic learning opportunities, and professional schools now compete internationally with public and private schools for the best students. However, these best students are not the typical white, middle-class high school graduates of twenty years ago. Universities are being required to do more by a much more diverse constituency. Middle- and upper-class high school graduates are becoming a minority in university classrooms. Today, students from industry/professional careers, returning students, international students, retirees, and other members of the public expect universities to be open and accessible to them. Many of these people do not fit traditional requirements for university admittance and compose a very different classroom with different needs and different expectations of university teaching and research.

The new developments in higher education mean that universities can no longer assume business as usual, and yet, most universities are still unprepared for a new kind of student or a different kind of research. As mentioned earlier, most universities do not even have a discourse that is accessible to the general public. As Bourdieu argues, even those disciplines that have purported to study humanity and human issues have developed such objective, theoretical, disinterested research that they have become isolated and distanced from the nonacademic problems of the people who are their subjects, communities, and constituencies. Inasmuch as this research has created its own unique academic discourse, so too has much of it isolated academic work from social relevance and from real activities of social action and social change.

As other institutions pull away from local action and community building, one of the ways in which universities can respond to their own identity struggles is by reintegrating themselves with their communities. This can be done through projects of social, organizational, and community change, like those described in this book. Community integration provides universities with multiple possibilities for both practical and theoretical learning. By learning how to read and write change—meaning, how to understand, interpret, and realign an organization's narratives and images—students, practitioners, and advocates of change can gain insights into power, social structures, individual agency, community agency, social change, and civic leadership. More pragmatically, by integrating university courses and faculty research with community development initiatives, students can learn important leadership skills, experience civic responsibility and community activism, become engaged in actual problems, and produce material that will have actual outcomes and actual consequences. Additionally, such work can teach students and faculty how to become effective and engaged agents of positive social change.

My hope is that readers of this book will be able to use the theory and the practices found in these chapters to build productive relationships between universities and community groups in their own academic fields and geographical locations. I hope that these relationships will help community groups and universities to create productive social changes, manage the changes that are occurring within their own organizations, and respond to the social changes that are happening in their local environments. As a guide for this future work, I would like to conclude by describing several additional successful ways in which community-minded academics have endeavored to link their own research and teaching with community development efforts. In each of these cases, teachers and researchers have chosen to become involved in their communities and actively respond to social problems, breaking with traditions of disinterested research and passive reporting. Cowen, in his own attempt to realign the academic community's images and narratives, notes that many universities are starting to realize that they can use their intellectual resources to help solve problems. Echoing Access Bank's future-past narrative, Cowen argues his own narrative, asserting that, "Academics are not, by their very nature, introverted and remote from reality; many . . . embrace the outside world, with all its faults, rather than retreat from the needs of society and want to be part of solving these problems."[10] Whether or not Cowen's assessment of academics is accurate is not really the issue. What is important is that he is articulating a new identity for academics and is engaged in the project of attempting to redefine who we are and what we do.

What should be stressed in each of these examples that follow are the ways these projects are partnerships between academics and community groups. As was more or less the case in my own work with MacKenzie College, Margaret's campaign, and Pleasant View Cemetery, these are not professors and students who enter foreign contexts with ready-made solutions and who force their own agendas on struggling communities. Again, it is important to recall that academics have very different ways of communicating, listening, and problem solving than those who work in nonacademic contexts. This does not mean that these two groups should not attempt to work together. However, it does mean that they must learn to recognize each other's unique contributions and perspectives. As Linda Flower, a professor at Carnegie Mellon University, has noted about her own work at the Pittsburgh-based Community Literacy Center, the strategies for communicating at the university and within the professional middle classes are radically different from those typically used in grassroots community organizations. She argues that all too often, academics and students enter a situation assuming that they already are experts.[11] Such a stance ignores each group's unique experiences, discourses, and problem-solving abilities.

Academics can be powerful resources in their ability to research and understand complex issues and in their ability to bring many different tools to the problem-solving table—in other words, in their ability to read a situation and then act on that reading. However, academics and students must resist those roles that cast them as experts ready to serve a needy constituency. Instead, both groups need to adopt the role of partners who are looking to solve problems with capable and experienced team-workers. In each of the examples that follow, academics have resisted the role of an expert and instead have found productive ways to work with groups and organizations in their communities.

Service Learning

At DePaul University, Roger Graves, an associate professor of English, has been a leading proponent of "service learning" courses. In these courses, students partner with community groups, not-for-profit companies, and other local organizations to produce real-world products that meet actual community needs. Recently, his students have worked with welfare-to-work programs, an employment center, preschool programming, an autistic children's support group, a residence for women recently released from prison, a neighborhood organization, and a public interest research group. When working with these organizations, Graves's students write to achieve very specific purposes: obtain funding for a service agency, distribute information about an agency to the public, or create identification within a community. The primary audience for these documents and tasks is not the professor but the clients outside of the classroom. In addition, the writing the students complete has actual consequences. These are not papers the teacher reads once and then hands back to the student; Graves's students have produced web sites, grant proposals, newsletters, brochures, and other kinds of useful communication products.

Throughout these courses, Graves attempts to match his own curricular requirements with the needs brought to him by his partnering agencies. When brought together, the course material and the service learning experience provide students with more than just the "theory of theory," as Bourdieu would say. The combination of theory with experience presents academic questions and issues within the practical context of community service and community problem solving. Graves has called this writing "transformative" because it evokes change on both theoretical and practical levels.[12] At a theoretical level, these writing tasks transform the ways his students think about professional and technical writing, the ways they think about their communities, and the ways they think about their own involvement within these communities. At a practical level, the students' writing can literally transform the organization, the community, and the relationship between this university and its local communities.

Service learning pedagogy borrows much from the work of John Dewey, Paulo Freire, and other educationalists who have called for a more experiential and politically active educational system. Dewey argued that experience cannot be cut away from student thinking and learning, and most of his educational writing focuses on the concept of experience in education. Dewey writes that "the first stage of contact" with anything new for people of any age must be hands-on and experiential. Learning becomes a process of discovery and enactment in which students wrestle with problems firsthand and find their own solutions and successes. Dewey even states that it is only in these situations that students will actually think and learn.[13]

But Dewey's educational position is equally a political statement. As Kurt Spellmeyer argues, Dewey never believed that the tradition of "disinterested" scholarship was truly critical. He saw academic disinterestedness as a political statement formed by a nineteenth-century social elite that saw its power fading in the face of social and economic change. For Dewey, education as both a practical and theoretical (reflective) project was society's principal means of change and transformation as it strived towards fundamentally more egalitarian social relations.[14] To take away the practical component of education is to take away students' abilities for social action and social change.

Dewey's political position is similar to Paulo Freire's, who argued that education suffers from "narration sickness," meaning an educational process in which instructors "fill" the students with information that is "detached from reality."[15] Freire calls this the "banking approach" to education, which "will never propose to students that they critically consider reality." Instead, this method deals with artificial and meaningless contexts that remove students from any engagement with their community or with social problems. As Freire has quipped, "It will deal instead with such vital questions as whether Roger gave green grass to the goat."[16]

In contrast, Freire calls for an educational experience that stresses "acts of cognition[,] not transferals of information."[17] Like

Graves's service learning classes, this pedagogy stresses problem-posing and dialogue between teachers and students who work together as "teacher-student" and "students-teachers." Freire writes that in such an environment, "the teacher is no longer merely the-one-who-teaches, but one who is [also] taught in dialogue with the students." Likewise, students take an active role in teaching and classroom instruction.[18] In a service learning context, teachers often include members of the community. The service learning curriculum is practical, as it is focused on action and on doing specific tasks that are directed towards the concrete needs of people in local communities. At the same time, the curriculum is theoretical, as it requires students to respond at an intellectual level to what they are seeing and experiencing.[19] At the intellectual level, critical reflection about the project and the context of service enables members of the class to recognize the ways social problems become naturalized into social structures and into individuals' own habitus. Participants can denaturalize these behaviors and examine how their own ritual behaviors and routines are complicit with oppressive and unjust social structures.

Thomas Huckin, a professor at the University of Utah, regularly offers service learning courses in partnership with the University of Utah's Lowell Bennion Community Service Center. Huckin argues that service learning courses should have three distinct goals: (1) helping students develop their academic skills, (2) helping students develop more civic awareness, and (3) helping the larger community by addressing the needs of local nonprofit agencies.[20] Huckin also argues that service learning projects should meet four other goals in order to be successful practically and pedagogically. The community service project must be relatively technical and must challenge students' abilities; it should be able to be accomplished within the limited time frame of the course; it should involve non-confidential information so that the project can be freely discussed in class; and it should be a priority for the partnering agency.[21] Finally, Huckin notes that the civic goals of service learning cannot occur unless class time is set aside for student reflection and discussion. Huckin argues that the goal of such a discussion should be to ask such questions as, "Why do nonprofit agencies like the

Battered Women's Shelter, Big Brothers and Big Sisters, Habitat for Humanity, and the Nature Conservancy exist in the first place?"[22]

As a pedagogy of action, service learning courses occupy a unique and problematic space in academic discussions. Some writers emphasize Marxist principles of work, labor, and value to discount service and experiential learning as nothing more than student exploitation and free labor. This argument suggests that community service only buys into capitalist economic models because it is too narrow in its approach. In other words, community service merely tinkers with economic disparities and teaches students that fundamentally there is nothing wrong with capitalism. Service learning does not encourage students to see social problems as larger structural economic problems requiring a new form of economic order. Even worse, critics state that such a model imposes exploitative capitalist relations on a classroom because students are not financially rewarded for the extra value they bring to and generate within their organizations. Other critics contend that schools and universities should play no role whatsoever in community service. These critics argue that the market must be left to regulate itself and sort out its winners and losers. Forcing students to volunteer outside of the classroom, these critics suggest, only takes away from real learning inside the classroom.

But such criticisms are increasingly hard to justify in the current context of university education. First, as Huckin notes, service learning, if nothing else, teaches students the importance of understanding the broader contexts involved in problem solving. By working within a diverse and distinct social context, students learn about the multiple factors that accompany social problems and how to consider the ways these factors intersect in social situations.[23] Second, writers who argue that service learning teaches students that there is nothing wrong with capitalism continue to assume passive, compliant students who are unable to make critical decisions and reach theoretically informed positions. Through discerning, self-reflective engagements with their experiences, students may come to any number of conclusions. Some may express a deep distrust with capitalist economics; others may not. What is important is not that students learn to parrot an instructor's ideological position.

Rather, it is important that through their experiences, students learn to construct their own political ideals and values and learn how to give voice to those values and enact their opinions. If, as Dewey suggests, education is a cornerstone of democracy, it is vital that students not be forced into accepting any one interpretation of their experience. The classroom must become a place not only for developing one's own political voice but also for learning tolerance, negotiation, and how to learn from another's experience. To force students into one interpretation is to deny them the richness of opinion that the university was founded to support. This is not to say that the classroom should become an uncritical or lazy intellectual environment. Rather, it needs to be a contested, empirical space where different opinions will struggle and connect as students and teachers learn from and interpret their research and experience.

Third, critics of service learning often place too much emphasis on the role of a paternalistic teacher who knows what is best for students and who must protect students from the ills of the nonacademic world. Again, not only does this perspective isolate students from their own learning but it distrusts any learning that is not officially sanctioned by the teacher. Such a pedagogy is essentially passive and fundamentally opposed to change. It teaches students to be complicit in the face of authority, to embrace the status quo, and not to seek interpretations, readings, or implications other than those offered by an authority. This leaves students unable to cope with change and unable to trust their own experiences and interpretations. Denying students the ability to act on their own leaves them continually looking to authority figures for validation and approval. As Astin and Astin argue, these messages are already too prevalent in a higher education system that emphasizes status-quo management and maintenance over leadership and change. In some ways, my own experience at MacKenzie College reinforces this point. The students at MacKenzie were never taught how to act as responsible agents of change; they never saw their own instructors adopt principles of change; and they were never involved in the management of the school as empowered participants. As a result, when they had problems, they did not have the managerial skills to act on those problems. Instead, they turned their hostility underground, and rather than work towards change, their stories and actions subverted the educational mission of the school.

This is not an issue of academic difficulty or intellectual rigor. If done properly, service learning courses should be equally or even more intellectually demanding and rigorous than classroom-specific courses. Not only must students learn fundamental principles but they must apply these principles to an actual setting. In addition, they must critically engage and critique their work and their activities in the class. The actual project should not stand alone but must be blended with specific learning objectives, outcomes assessment, and student expectations.

Fourth, enacting community service is no more a form of exploitation than forcing students to compose essays on topics they do not care about or to write research papers no one will ever read. Recalling Foucault's argument about institutions and their normalizing role in society, one could argue that all education is fundamentally exploitative because it forces people to submit themselves to relations of power and authority. Those who argue that service learning is exploitative are more plausibly arguing against its practice-based curriculum. These critiques again emphasize the academic culture of disinterested analysis and reveal a deeply held bias against practical action. Thus, when writers argue against student exploitation, they will usually argue in favor of specific readings, books, lectures, and content that students must learn—again demonstrating a deeply rooted form of pedagogical paternalism and a distrust of experiential learning and change.

Oddly enough, the greatest challenge facing service learning projects is a lack of opportunities for student projects. This challenge is especially great in rural communities that do not have a large population base. In many communities throughout North America, few people are aware of service learning classes, and even fewer know how to partner with university courses. Few community groups are even aware that such opportunities exist. For example, Andrew, the manager of Pleasant View Cemetery, did not realize that he could get students at the local university to help him with his web site or his promotional materials.

In order to enable the continued success of service learning programs, university administrators and faculty need to develop ways to promote and link these classes within the local community. At the same time, community groups need to approach university leaders, department chairs, and individual faculty members in order to help organize and plan potential courses. Although the best links between university courses and communities emerge from and respond to local contexts and issues, there are several things that can be done to help foster such contacts:

- Student scholarships and financial aid packages could be targeted towards students who are involved in community projects and who demonstrate civic leadership.
- Faculty could be given reduced teaching loads if they are employing service learning practices in the classroom. This incentive will enable faculty to better administer these courses, build stronger community connections, and plan future courses.
- Faculty could be given paid sabbaticals to work for nonprofits and community groups.
- Community service could play a greater role in decisions on faculty promotion and tenure.
- Following the lead of the Lowell Bennion Community Service Center at the University of Utah, universities could establish community outreach centers to help link student and faculty initiatives with community and civic groups.
- Foundations and philanthropic organizations could provide small grants to help service learning courses with start-up expenses and overhead expenses incurred by students throughout their projects (mailing, photocopying, travel, publishing).
- Foundations could provide grants that enable faculty to spend an academic year with a nonprofit organization.
- Admissions decisions could place greater emphasis on community service
- Grassroots community leaders could plan regular meetings with faculty and university departments to discuss curriculum ideas, service learning opportunities, and other points of intersection between the community and the academy.
- Civic workers and grassroots leaders could be appointed to university boards of directors and could be awarded honorary Ph.D.'s or other university awards.
- Academic journals could foster more publications on service learning and community action through special issues, calls for papers, and special forums.

- Universities could make their facilities more available to community groups for meetings, conferences, workshops, and other events.
- Community groups could approach academic departments about offering summer workshops, special courses, or guest lectures on issues like proposal writing, business plans, change management, accounting, fund-raising, or market research.

Action Research

The Digital Clubhouse is a community center located in a mall in Sunnyvale, California. Here, volunteers teach Clubhouse participants how to use digital, multimedia technologies by creating CD-ROM autobiographies.[24] Working together, the volunteer experts and Clubhouse participants write narratives, create storyboards, scan pictures, and create and download videos as they place their life stories on CD-ROM for easy retrieval and presentation. The Digital Clubhouse's signature program is called "Producing the Producers." Once a participant has created a "digital story," that person becomes responsible for helping two more people to complete two new story projects. Those two new storytellers must each recruit and train two more storytellers, and so on. The Clubhouse recently presented a World War II project in which veterans presented their life stories to Sunnyvale residents. In addition to this project, the Clubhouse is producing life stories that focus on women's issues, stories by cancer patients that tell of their experiences living with cancer, and stories by disabled adults. As participants document their stories, they also learn basics of technical communication, internet technology, word processing software, project management, and other job-related skills.

At first glance, projects like the Digital Clubhouse appear to be solely community service activities. But according to a growing group of academics, such projects could be considered academic research. Community-based action research is an outgrowth of early models of anthropological, ethnographic research that tried to resolve social problems practically. Ernest Stringer writes that early forms of action research suffered a decline because of their association with "radical political activism" in the 1960s. However, community-based action research has recently reemerged as a more disciplined inquiry, closely connected to practitioner research, new paradigm research, and teacher-as-researcher research. Stringer notes that community-based action research seeks to improve the quality of people's lives by fully engaging subjects "as equal and full participants in the research process."[25] This research begins with an interest in the problems of a community group, and its purpose is to help people understand and resolve the social problems that they face. Stringer writes, "Community-based action research provides a model for enacting local, action-oriented approaches to inquiry, applying small-scale theorizing to specific problems in specific situations."[26]

Likewise, Egon Guba has argued that community-based action research exhibits three important characteristics of human inquiry: "decentralization, deregulation, and cooperativeness in execution."[27] By decentralization, Guba means research that is interested in emphasizing local contexts and local knowledge rather than in trying to uncover generalizable truths and universal narratives. By deregulation, he means a concern "away from the restrictive conventional rules of the research game, the overweening concern with validity, reliability, objectivity, and generalizability."[28] Guba argues that in the realm of human inquiry, such concerns are "simply irrelevant" because what most social researchers study depends on individuals' mental constructions and interpretations, concepts that elide quantitative measurements. Finally, by cooperativeness in execution, Guba means a type of research that blurs the typical distinction between the researcher and the researched.

Although they are not ideal examples of the kinds of research Stringer and Guba recommend, the research projects reported in this book look to community-based action research as a productive model. Stringer writes that ideally, such research should be "democratic . . . equitable . . . liberating . . . and life enhancing—it should enable the expression of people's full human potential."[29] These are high goals for social research. Noting that traditional research projects attempt to uncover, or record, with the ultimate goal of publication, Stringer writes that, while community-based action research may also result in publication and theorization, "its primary purpose is a practical tool for solving problems experienced

by people in their professional, community, or private lives." If a
research project "does not make a difference in a specific way," he
writes, "then it has failed to achieve its objectives."[30]

In addition to the projects discussed in the previous chapters,
a useful example of community-based action research can be found
in C. Kenneth Banks and J. Marshall Mangan's *The Company of
Neighbours: Revitalizing Community Through Action-Research*.
Banks and Mangan report on their work with a locally managed,
nonprofit community association called The Company of Neighbours in Hespler, Ontario. The project was originated as both a
community association and a research project and was an attempt,
in the words of Banks and Mangan, "to move away from the kinds
of outside-influenced, highly structured programs that have come
to characterize much of the social work directed at individuals,
families, and groups in the past."[31] The practical purpose of the
project was to establish mutual-aid relationships among people in
the Hespler area, a small city experiencing social and economic
decline. The project unfolded as the principal researchers undertook
information gathering, consultation, and the facilitation of local
initiatives. These researchers write that they did not use the community to test hypotheses or implement predesigned programs.
Everything they did emerged from local input and feedback. This
required a flexible and responsive research plan as the researchers
continually altered their project and research design as new information and new ideas emerged.

Banks and Mangan note that action research is not an entirely
new phenomenon. They cite Myles Horton's work with the High-
lander Schools in Tennessee, which provided education to miners
and trade unionists and was deeply involved in the United States'
civil rights struggles.[32] Banks and Mangan also discuss the rural
education efforts of Father Moses Coady and others at St. Francis
Xavier University. Through the university's extension department,
these local activists helped thousands of people in rural Nova Scotia
build cooperative business models and credit unions. Although
Banks and Mangan note that this work was still informed by a
prevalent "missionary attitude," they argue that more recent forms

of action research, led by educators like Freire, have developed stronger and more thorough critical and theoretical analyses and a greater emphasis on partnerships and dialogical (dialogue-based) meaning making.

Finally, Dennis Sumara and Terrance Carson argue that action research enfolds epistemological concerns (how one comes to know reality) with ontological concerns (the nature of reality). As Sumara and Carson write: "Who one is becomes completely caught up in what one knows and does. . . . What is thought, what is represented, what is acted upon, are all intertwined aspects of lived experience and, as such, cannot be discussed or interpreted separately."[33] Thus, the knowledge produced by action research cannot be considered apart from its historical, political, cultural, social, and personal contexts. It has emerged from a specific situation in order to influence and change that situation.

Despite the ways it brings the university and the community together, community-based action research has a long way to go before it can be considered mainstream academic research. First, in addition to its alternative assumptions about practice, theory, and objective inquiry, action research also presents researchers with challenges to data collection, reporting, and generalizable theorizing. Because action researchers are deeply involved as participants in the events of their research, they will find it more difficult to record information from colleagues, clients, and other stakeholders who are unfamiliar with data collection. Some participants may be unwilling to turn meetings into data collection sessions. Other stakeholders may be unwilling to volunteer some kinds of information to people who are involved as participants in the project. In addition, action research poses some problems related to sharing confidential information or, in some cases, proprietary information.

Second, action research has few outlets for academic publication. Not many academic journals publish action research. In my own fields of business and technical communications and rhetoric and composition, there have been few, if any, action research articles published in leading journals. Since university researchers are dependent on publication for promotion and tenure decisions, a lack of publishing outlets and opportunities for action research seriously impedes faculty initiatives in community action. In addition, action research (like other forms of ethnography) requires a considerable amount of time and may not lead to immediately publishable results. In some cases, action research may take several years before a project is developed enough to publish. Given these limitations on time and publishing, action research and community action is an extremely risky, if not impossible, endeavor for junior, untenured faculty. As a consequence, these institutional and professional structures work to actively dissuade faculty from becoming agents of change within their academic and local communities.

Universities and academic disciplines that seek more interaction with their communities need to better support and encourage forms of community-based action research. Again, some of the best ways to do this will emerge from local and discipline-specific discussions. However, several initiatives could include the following:

- Academic journals could be more aware of action research as a unique and valuable area of scholarly activity. Rather than marginalize action research because it is participatory and engaged in its research context, journals could adopt standards for reviewing and writing appropriate peer-reviewed action research.
- Research foundations and other philanthropic organizations could highlight and sponsor action research projects. Foundations could include action research in their calls for proposals and in position statements.
- Community groups could consider using forms of action research to solve problems or improve their organizations. When working with academics, these organizations could better consider and make arrangements for the academic, research-specific needs of faculty.
- Faculty could include action research components in more traditional research proposals. When designing a research project, faculty could consider potential community applications or projects that could enhance or apply research.
- Universities could create community partnerships through their research offices to encourage action research and match faculty with appropriate community needs.
- Grassroots organizations could meet with university research

offices to discuss potential projects, community needs, and faculty interests.

- Junior faculty could be given incentives to work on action research so that such projects would not jeopardize tenure and promotion possibilities.

Writing for a Broader Audience

A third way to build academic and community partnerships involves the ways academics report scholarly research. Writing more accessible prose, either through creative nonfiction, journalism, editorial writing, expert commentary, or popular books, places academic conversations within larger and potentially more influential contexts and communities. In a presentation to the Association of Teachers of Technical Writing, my colleague Stephen Doheny-Farina argued that our relevance as teachers and subject-matter experts has little to do with how influential we are within our own disciplines but how influential we are in other communities.[34] He noted that in a recent sociological study, Lee Ben Clarke argues that very little scholarly work has been done in the area of audience reception and audience awareness.[35] Doheny-Farina's audience, experts in technical and scientific writing, knew that this claim represented a huge academic oversight—scholars in this field have studied audience awareness, text reception, and cognitive and social conditions of audiences since before Clarke was born. However, Doheny-Farina said that academic indignation is the wrong response to this issue. Instead, he said that people in technical writing need to reexamine the ways they publish and disseminate knowledge and ask themselves how someone working in the area of public rhetoric could complete a full study of this topic without once encountering their field.

Doheny-Farina's questions apply to more disciplines than just technical communications. Throughout this book, I have been critical of academic conventions that result in books, journal articles, and conference presentations that are not accessible to their own subject populations. Understandably, such criticism has its limitations. For example, one would not expect a study of first graders' reading abilities to be fully comprehensible to first graders. However, it would not be unrealistic for this material to be comprehensible and available to the children's teacher, their parents, or curriculum planners. Similarly, studies of workplaces, community groups, cooperatives, and other adult environments could be made more accessible to the populations who enabled such research in the first place. For example, in preparing this book, Neil, Margaret, and Andrew were all consulted on the "readability" of the text. I also asked several other nonacademics to read the text and assist me with its development. This is not to say that this book is perfectly legible for all audiences. Undoubtedly, some will argue that there are passages here that are too academic, unnecessarily burdensome, or too complex.

But I do not want to argue that academics must abandon academic writing and disciplinary communication. Nor do I want to suggest that we simply "dumb down" our work for a generalist audience. As an advocate of lifelong learning, I hope that the books I read improve my vocabulary, sharpen my critical skills, and continue to push and pull me along their way. Just as medical and legal discourses support and build their respective communities, so too does academic discourse play an important organizational role within specific disciplinary communities. At the same time, we need to be aware of our narratives and our images. When we focus on our own academic discourse, we strengthen our community narratives and our perceptions of ourselves. However, at the same time, we risk becoming parochial and insular if we alienate other stakeholders and other potential readers. Publishing in nondisciplinary forums serves the important organizational role of image-building. External publications show people outside of our own discipline what we are doing, what our research is producing, what we have found, and where we are going. It builds a larger community of stakeholders and builds a larger audience for our research. Image-building, through wider publication strategies, is directly tied to the future success of our disciplines and our universities as it influences our ability to secure research grants, gain access to research sites, attract students, and ultimately create change within our universities and our communities.

There are many different ways to bring academic research to a more general, public audience. Some suggested initiatives could include the following:

- Departments and disciplinary committees could recognize the value of external publications in tenure and promotion decisions.
- University departments could discuss ways to promote their research activities in community publications.
- Academic journals could be more receptive to nonacademic authors.
- Scholars could find and learn more about alternative forums for publishing research.
- Popular forums (magazines, newspapers, electronic sites) could partner with academic communities to develop strategies for peer review and validation.
- Academic journals and presses could be more receptive to genres that attempt to cross disciplinary/community boundaries (creative nonfiction, action research).
- Faculty could coauthor research material with community participants.
- Academic journals could include community members or other stakeholders on peer review boards.
- Faculty could become more involved in nondisciplinary review boards and nondisciplinary publishing ventures.
- Graduate students could be encouraged to write for both popular and discipline-specific forums.
- Graduate students could learn how to promote their research in newspapers and other forms of public media.
- Academic conferences could include presentations from and discussions with stakeholder groups, community participants, and research participants.

Springtime

One spring morning, Mr. Wolouski walked over from his front yard to inspect my lawn and watch me wash my car. He liked watching me work, not because I was particularly efficient but because he knew it unnerved me. He would stand on the sidewalk and simply watch as I washed down the side doors, scrubbed off bits of asphalt and grit, and then rinsed away the soap and mud. The first couple of times he came over I waved and kinked the hose, expecting a short chat or a story. But he would not oblige. He was "just watching," he'd say. So, I learned that for him, a simple nod is words enough, and I kept to my business.

But this day was different. Today he wanted me to help him prune his apple tree. Mrs. Wolouski wanted it cut short; she thought it looked messy and was about to get hung up on the cable line. He wanted it left a little longer. He enjoyed the privacy and the shade it gave him when he worked in the garden. I turned off the hose and left the still dirty car, knowingly walking into another Wolouski family quarrel. After a good hour of scratches, punctures, an occasional misstep, and a few minor injuries, my err(or) was about halfway between the Wolouskis' competing visions. And, as expected, both parties condemned me for doing a lousy job.

Looking back at that particular story, I realize that it did not matter how long or short I cut that tree. The morning's activities were not about pruning tree branches; they were about reconciliation, about personal identities, and about change. Reading and writing change represent more than a way to interpret organizational transformations and social change. They represent a different kind of scholarship and a different kind of writing, a story that is politically engaged and socially active, a story that realizes limitations but is not afraid to recommend action, one that can entertain while still inform, one that emerges from the familiar, the everyday, and even the mundane.

These are the stories waiting to be changed, and these are the changes out there waiting to be storied. Stories of image, narrative, and identity, how we bring these concepts together and how we will use them to change our communities, our organizations, and ourselves—that, of course (and predictably), is the next story.

- NOTES
- BIBLIOGRAPHY
- INDEX

NOTES

1. Introduction: Rodeo

1. Davis and Botkin, 1994, p. 15.

2. Hanna and Associates, 2000, p. 14.

3. Meister, 1998, p. 208.

4. Aronowitz, 2000, p. xviii.

5. This separation between the theoretical and the practical has not remain unopposed. See, e.g., Segal, Paré, Brent, and Vipond, 1998, for an account of their work as consultants to business and industry and the ways these researchers have attempted to bridge workplace and academic contexts.

6. Van Maanen, 1988, pp. 73–74 (confessional), 101–2 (impressionist).

7. Van Maanen, 1988, pp. 75–77.

8. Van Maanen, 1988, pp. 101–3.

9. Van Maanen, 1988, p. 105.

10. Van Maanen, 1988, p. 105.

11. Cintron, 1997, pp. 8–9.

12. Scheper-Hughes, 1992, p. 18.

13. Herndl and Nahrwold, 2000, p. 260; Schwandt, 1994, p. 119.

14. Herndl and Nahrwold cite various researchers in technical and professional writing whose work offers direct political challenges (2000, pp. 277–83). See also Selfe and Selfe, 1996; Sullivan and Porter, 1997.

15. Goodall, 1994, p. xiii.

16. Goodall, 1994, p. xiii.

17. Barthes, 1975, p. 47.

2. Reading the Stories of Change

1. Rosenblatt, 1999.

2. Rosenblatt, 1999.

3. Burrell and Morgan, 1979, p. 50.

4. Hyman, 1995.

5. Hyman, 1995, pp. 42–43.

6. Hyman, 1995, p. 43.

7. Heath, 1994, p. 5.

8. Fairclough, 1992, p. 64.

9. Heath argues that "each organization exists as communication" (1994, p. 21) and that the communication people perform at work creates their organizations. Empirically, Sullivan (1997) has shown how opposing discourses communicated in contrasting versions of tax manuals at an IRS Service Center created a contradictory and dysfunctional work environment. Winsor has argued that within organizations, "writing is visibly used not just to record decisions and events but to do the organization's work, to build its shared understanding, and to construct its knowledge" (1989, p. 271). Winsor's essay demonstrates how corporate writing establishes shared knowledge within the organization and thus shapes and forms meaning within the corporation (p. 282). For other discussions of the social roles written communication plays within organizational settings, see Blyler and Thralls, 1993; Duin and Hansen, 1996; and Spilka, 1993.

10. Mumby, 1993, p. 5. See also Mumby, 1987, and 1988. Blyler has repeatedly shown the cultural roles narratives play within professional contexts. She has argued that in classroom settings, teachers can use narrative as a way of focusing student discussions of professional texts on issues of power and control (1995). In research settings, she has argued that narratives and the study of narratives have often been devalued in studies of professional communication (1996). Although she profiles various narrative writers and advocates of narratives, Blyler's own work is not narrative. For Blyler, and other writers on narrative in the field of business communication (Jameson, 2000), narratives are ways non-experts interpret their workplace, read workplace texts, and interpret the social significance of business communication. However, narratives are rarely viewed as an appropriate way of writing or reporting academic research.

11. Mumby, 1993, p. 5.

12. Mumby, 1993, p. 3; 1987, pp. 118, 125.

13. Heath, 1994, p. 60.

14. Kerby, 1991, p. 53.

15. Berkenkotter and Huckin, 1995, pp. 111–13, 115.

16. Bourdieu, 1992.

17. Dutton and Dukerich (1981) have also tied the concept of image to organizational identity. In a more recent paper, Dutton, Dukerich, and Harquail (1994) reassert this connection to argue that image integrates a person's internal and external perception of the organization. As Dutton,

Dukerich, and Harquail note, image reflects the extent to which people will define themselves as part of their organization. My use of image extends Dutton, Dukerich, and Harquail's concept; however, I use image to describe a more distant concept—that to which the organization aspires or, in the case of a dysfunctional organization, that which the organization is forced to become (see chapter 5).

18. Morgan, 1986, p. 256.

19. Casey, 1995, p. 109.

20. See http://info.nike.com; www.saigon.com; www.devp.org; www.caa.org.au/campaigns/nike/index.html.

21. Aristotle, 1991.

22. Cherry, 1988, p. 253.

23. Hatch, 1996, p. 31.

24. Grossberg, 1994, p. 15. For other arguments about the heterogeneity of identity and the ability to switch between multiple subject positions, see Hall and Held, 1990; Giroux, 1994.

25. Fairclough, 1992, p. 90.

26. Hammer and Stanton, 1995, p. 178.

27. Johansen and Swigart, 1994.

28. Tomasko, 1993, p. 23.

29. Tomasko, 1996. Tomasko's story gets even more interesting. The former proponent of change-management-as-downsizing now leads full- or half-day "Go for Growth" management workshops. In a biographical sketch about Tomasko, Celebrity Speakers International Limited writes that he "challenges managers to commit their businesses to continued growth, rather than a seemingly endless series of cycles of cost cutting and restructuring. He shows alternative strategies for business growth and outlines how individuals and organizations can benefit from this approach" (http://www.speakers.co.uk/5001.htm).

30. Heath, 1994, p. 88.

31. Heath, 1994, p. 89.

3. Time, Habits, and Change: Brokers, Bankers, and the Old West

1. McMurtry, 1999, p. 188.

2. Rogers, 1993, p. 9.

3. Rogers, 1993, p. 2.

4. Christophe, 1974.

5. Rose, 1987, p. 330.

6. Compton, 1987, p. xiii.

7. Compton, 1987, p. 19.

8. Editorial, 1984, p. 3.

9. For reasons of confidentiality, citations referring to the actual bank have been withheld.

10. Bourdieu, 1990b, p. 53. A note on the use of the word "uncon-

scious": Bourdieu writes that "the 'unconscious' is never anything other than the forgetting of history which history itself produces by incorporating the objective structures it produces in the second natures of habitus," by which he means the systematic, taken-for-granted aspects of past events. Bourdieu writes of "yesterday's man" who "predominates" in us, yet we do not sense him because he is inveterate, or confirmed in our habits. See Bourdieu, 1977, pp. 78–79.

11. Giddens, 1984, p. 376.

12. Giddens, 1991, pp. 199, 204.

13. Giddens, 1991, pp. 12, 184–85.

14. Gasparino, 1996, p. C1.

15. Gasparino, 1996, p. C1.

16. Gasparino, 1996, p. C1.

17. Information on the town can be found at http://www.ghosttowns. com/states/ut/ophir.html.

18. See http://www.ghosttowns.com/states/ut/mercur.html.

19. Giddens, 1991, p. 215.

20. Giddens writes, "To know the meaning of words is thus to be able to use them as an integral part of the routine enactment of day-to-day life" (1991, p. 43).

21. Gee, Hull, and Lankshear, 1996, pp. 24–48 (chap. 2).

22. Examples of "fast capitalist texts" cited by Gee, Hull, and Lankshear include Boyett and Conn, 1992; Peters, 1992; Senge, 1990; and Hammer and Champy, 1993. See also Johansen and Swigart, 1994; and Tomasko, 1987, 1993.

23. Castells, 1993, pp. 15–17; Gee, Hull, and Lankshear, 1996, pp. 36–42. See also Reich, 1992; and Johnson-Eilola, 1996. Johnson-Eilola uses Reich's description of "symbolic-analytic work" to argue that technical communicators play a pivotal role as information managers in a postindustrial economy.

24. Gee, Hull, and Lankshear, 1996, p. xv.

25. Gee, Hull, and Lankshear, 1996, p. xvi.

26. Gee, Hull, and Lankshear, 1996, pp. 156–58.

27. Gee, Hull, and Lankshear, 1996, p. 32.

28. Gee, Hull, and Lankshear, 1996, p. 166.

29. Gee, Hull, and Lankshear, 1996, p. 143.

4. Narratives and Organizational Change: Stories from Academe

1. Willis, 1977.

2. Giroux, 1983.

3. Fairclough, 1992, p. 58.

4. Foucault, 1970, pp. 386–87.

5. Macey, 1993, pp. 190, 215. See also Simons, 1995. Simons writes:

"Foucault's oppositional politics is posed in substantially negative terms. There is no plea here for new subjectivities, but a critique of the contemporary subject and its conditions of possibility" (p. 50). Further, Simons notes, "Rather than attempting to provide political answers, Foucault wishes to 'question politics' along lines that 'are not determined by a pre-established political outlook and do not tend toward the realization of some definite political project'" (p. 50; original citation, Foucault, 1984, p. 375). Foucault was not interested in proposing alternatives to given or existent systems, claiming that such a project was "tiresome," since to "imagine another system is to extend our participation in the present system" (Simons, 1995, p. 50; original citation, Foucault, 1977, p. 230).

6. For a review of Foucault's work applied to organizations and institutions, see Burrell, 1988.

7. See Foucault, 1983; Moore, 1987; Simons, 1995, pp. 34–36.

8. Foucault, 1973.

9. Foucault, 1994; 1979; 1978.

10. Foucault, 1979, p. 228.

11. Foucault, 1972, p. 166.

12. Foucault, 1972, p. 31.

13. Macey, 1993, p. 202.

14. Simons, 1995, pp. 26–27.

15. Foucault, 1972, pp. 168, 171, 172, 173.

16. Lewis and Smith, 1994, p. 4.

17. Davis and Botkin, 1994, p. 15.

18. Davis and Botkin, 1994, p. 16.

19. Moore, 1997, pp. 77–85.

5. Image: Power, Rhetoric, and Change

1. Foucault, 1979, p. 228.

2. Foucault, 1979, p. 194.

3. Simons, 1995, p. 82.

4. Fairclough, 1992, pp. 37–61; Giddens, 1984, pp. 256–58.

5. Giddens, 1984, p. 258.

6. Giddens, 1979, p. 114.

7. Giddens, 1984, pp. 258–59.

8. Boyne, 1991, p. 57.

9. Boyne, 1991, p. 67.

10. See the discussion of image in chapter 2.

11. Rottenberg, 1994, pp. 4–5.

6. Discordance and Realignment: Stories from the Final Frontier

1. Bledstein, 1976, p. 34.

2. Mitford, 1963; 1997, p. 116.

3. Mitford, 1997, p. 116.
4. Berkenkotter and Huckin, 1995, p. 18.
5. Giddens, 1979, p. 114.
6. Macey, 1993, p. 186.
7. Bourdieu, 1977, pp. 1–2.
8. Bourdieu, 1998, p. 130.
9. Bourdieu, 1990, p. 11.
10. Bourdieu, 1990, p. 11.
11. Bourdieu, 1977, p. 2.
12. Postone, LiPuma, and Calhoun, 1993, p. 3.
13. Bourdieu, 1990, pp. 62, 63.
14. Postone, LiPuma, and Calhoun, 1993, p. 4.
15. Postone, LiPuma, and Calhoun, 1993, p. 5.
16. Stuart Culver and I began using the phrase "distressed discourse" when referring to an organization that was no longer able to sustain a narrative or an image. I remember that the phrase first emerged after he read an early draft of this chapter.

7. Organizational Change as Community Action

1. Dias, Freedman, Medway, and Paré, 1999, pp. 222–23.
2. Dias, Freedman, Medway, and Paré, 1999, pp. 222–23.
3. Putnum, 2000.
4. Banks and Mangan, 1999, p. 3.
5. Astin and Astin, 2000, p. 2.
6. Astin and Astin, 2000, pp. 2–3.
7. Astin and Astin, 2000, p. 8.
8. Astin and Astin, 2000, pp. 3–4.
9. Cowen, 2000.
10. Cowen, 2000, 5.
11. Flower, 1998, p. 309.
12. Graves, forthcoming.
13. Dewey, 1985, pp. 160, 167.
14. Spellmeyer, 1993, p. 12; Dewey, 1985, pp. 368–69.
15. Freire, 1973, p. 57.
16. Freire, 1973, p. 61.
17. Freire, 1973, p. 67.
18. Freire, 1973, p. 67.
19. Freire, 1973, p. 85.
20. Huckin, 1997, p. 50.
21. Huckin, 1997, pp. 51–52.
22. Huckin, 1997, p. 58.
23. Huckin, 1997, p. 58.
24. Abdulezer, 2000; see also http://www.digiclub.org.

25. Stringer, 1996, p. 9; Calhoun, 1993.

26. Stringer, 1996, p. 9.

27. Guba, 1996, p. ix.

28. Guba, 1996, p. x.

29. Stringer, 1996, p. 10.

30. Stringer, 1996, p. 11.

31. Banks and Mangan, 1999, p. 4.

32. Banks and Mangan, 1999, p. 23; Horton, 1990; Horton and Freire, 1990.

33. Sumara and Carson, 1997, p. xvii; Guba, 1996, p. x.

34. Doheny-Farina, 2000.

35. Clarke, 1999.

BIBLIOGRAPHY

Abdulezer, S. 2000. A community of stories. *Converge Magazine* 3 (1): 62–68.

Aristotle. 1991. *On rhetoric: A theory of civil discourse.* Ed. and trans. George A. Kennedy. New York: Oxford University Press.

Aronowitz, S. 2000. *The knowledge factory: Dismantling the corporate university and creating true higher learning.* Boston: Beacon Press.

Astin, A., and H. Astin. 2000. *Leadership reconsidered: Engaging higher education in social change.* Battle Creek, MI: W. K. Kellogg Foundation.

Banks, C. K., and J. M. Mangan. 1999. *The company of neighbours: Revitalizing community through action-research.* Toronto: University of Toronto Press.

Barthes, R. 1975. *Pleasure of the text.* Trans. R. Miller. New York: Noonday.

Bemowski, K. 1991. Restoring the pillars of higher education. *Quality Progress* 24 (10): 37–42.

Berkenkotter, C., and T. Huckin. 1995. *Genre knowledge in disciplinary communities: Cognition/culture/power.* Hillsdale, NJ: Lawrence Erlbaum.

Bledstein, B. 1976. *The culture of professionalism: The middle class and the development of higher education in America.* New York: W. W. Norton.

Blyler, N. 1995. Pedagogy and social action: A role for narrative in professional communication. *Journal of Business and Technical Communication* 9 (3): 298–320.

———. 1996. Narrative and research in professional communication. *Journal of Business and Technical Communication* 10 (3): 330–51.

Blyler, N., and C. Thralls, eds. 1993. *Professional communication: The social perspective*. Newbury Park, CA: Sage.

Bourdieu, P. 1977. Reprint. *Outline of a theory of practice*. Trans. R. Nice. Cambridge, UK: Cambridge University Press. Original edition, Paris: Droz, 1972.

———. 1990a. *In other words: Essays towards a reflexive sociology*. Trans. M. Adamson. Stanford: Stanford University Press.

———. 1990b. Reprint. *The logic of practice*. Trans. R. Nice. Stanford: Stanford University Press. Original edition, Paris: Les Editions de Minuit, 1980.

———. 1992. *Language and symbolic power*. Ed. J. B. Thompson. Trans. G. Raymond and M. Adamson. Cambridge, UK: Polity.

———. 1998. *Practical reason: On the theory of action*. Stanford: Stanford University Press.

Boyett, J., and H. Conn. 1992. *Workplace 2000: The revolution reshaping American business*. New York: Plume/Penguin.

Boyne, R. 1991. Power-knowledge and social theory: The systematic misrepresentation of contemporary French social theory in the work of Anthony Giddens. In *Giddens' theory of structuration: A critical appreciation,* ed. C. Bryant and D. Jary. London: Routledge.

Burrell, G. 1988. Modernism, postmodernism and organizational analysis II: The contribution of Michel Foucault. *Organization Studies* 9 (2): 221–35.

Burrell, G., and G. Morgan. 1979. *Sociological paradigms and organizational analysis: Elements of the sociology of corporate life*. London: Heinemann.

Calhoun, E. 1993. Action research: Three approaches. *Educational Leadership* (October): 62–65.

Casey, C. 1995. *Work, self and society: After industrialism*. London: Routledge.

Castells, M. 1993. The information economy and the new international division of labor. In *The new global economy in the information age: Reflections on our changing world,* ed. M. Carnoy, M. Castells, S. Cohen, and F. Cardoso. University Park: Pennsylvania State University Press.

Cherry, R. 1988. Ethos versus persona: Self-representation in written discourse. *Written Communication* 5 (3): 251–76.

Christophe, C. 1974. *Competition in financial services*. New York: First National City Corporation.

Cintron, R. 1997. *Angels' town*. Boston: Beacon Press.

Clarke, L. B. 1999. *Mission improbable: Using fantasy documents to tame disasters*. Chicago: University of Chicago Press.

Compton, E. 1987. *The new world of commercial banking*. Lexington, MA: Lexington Books.

Cowen, S. 2000. Looking into the crystal ball: Opportunities and challenges for higher education. Presentation, CASE Conference on Corporate and Foundation Fundraising, July 11, Los Angeles.

Davis, S., and J. Botkin. 1994. *The monster under the bed.* New York: Simon and Schuster.

Debs, M. 1993. Reflexive and reflective tensions: Considering research methods from writing-related fields. In *Writing in the workplace: New research perspectives,* ed. R. Spilka. Carbondale: Southern Illinois University Press.

Dewey, J. 1985. *Democracy and education.* Ed. J. Boydston. Carbondale: Southern Illinois University Press.

Dias, P., A. Freedman, P. Medway, and A. Paré. 1999. *Worlds apart: Acting and writing in academic and workplace contexts.* Mahwah, NJ: Lawrence Erlbaum.

Doheny-Farina, S. 2000. Keynote address, Association of Teachers of Technical Writing Annual Conference, April 12, Minneapolis, MN.

Duin, A. H., and C. Hansen, eds. 1996. *Nonacademic writing: Social theory and technology.* Mahwah, NJ: Lawrence Erlbaum.

Dutton, I. E., and J. M. Dukerich. 1981. Keeping an eye on the mirror: Image and identity in organizational adaptation. *Academy of Management Journal* 34 (3): 517–54.

Dutton, I. E., J. M. Dukerich, and C. V. Harquail. 1994. Organizational images and member identification. *Administrative Science Quarterly* 39 (2): 239–63.

Fairclough, N. 1992. *Discourse and social change.* Cambridge, UK: Polity.

Flower, L. 1998. *Problem solving strategies for writing in college and community.* New York: Harcourt Brace.

Foucault, M. 1970. Reprint. *The order of things: An archaeology of the human sciences.* New York: Random House. Original edition, Paris: Editions Gallimard, 1966.

———. 1972. Reprint. *The archaeology of knowledge and The discourse on language.* Trans. A. Sheridan Smith. New York: Pantheon. Original editions, Paris: Editions Gallimard, 1969, 1971.

———. 1973. Reprint. *Madness and civilization: A history of insanity in the age of reason.* Trans. R. Howard. New York: Vintage. Original edition, Paris: Plon, 1961.

———. 1977. Revolutionary action: Until now. In *Language, counter-memory, practice: Selected essays and interviews,* ed. D. Bouchard; trans. D. Bouchard and S. Simon. Ithaca: Cornell University Press.

———. 1978. Reprint. *The history of sexuality: An introduction.* Trans. R. Hurley. Harmondsworth: Penguin. Original edition, Paris: Gallimard, 1976.

———. 1979. *Discipline and punish: The birth of the prison.* Trans. A.

Sheridan. New York: Vintage. Original edition, Paris: Editions Gallimard, 1975.

———. 1983. On the genealogy of ethics: An overview of work in progress. In *The Foucault reader,* ed. P. Rabinow; trans. C. Porter. New York: Pantheon.

———. 1984. Politics and ethics: An overview. In *The Foucault reader,* ed. Paul Rabinow; trans. C. Porter. New York: Pantheon.

———. 1994. Reprint. *The birth of the clinic: An archaeology of medical perception.* Trans. A. Sheridan Smith. New York: Vintage. Original edition, Paris: Presses Universitaires de France, 1963.

Freire, P. 1973. Reprint. *Pedagogy of the oppressed.* Trans. M. Ramos. New York: Seabury Press. Original manuscript (in Portuguese), 1968.

Frost, P., et al., eds. 1985. *Organizational culture: The meaning of life in the workplace.* Beverly Hills, CA: Sage.

Gasparino, C. 1996. Banks are found lacking in mutual-fund disclosures. *Wall Street Journal,* January 16, C1.

Gee, J., G. Hull, and C. Lankshear. 1996. *The new work order: Behind the language of the new capitalism.* Boulder, CO: Westview.

Giddens, A. 1979. *Central problems in social theory: Action, structure and contradiction in social analysis.* Berkeley: University of California Press.

———. 1984. *The constitution of society: Outline of a theory of structuration.* Berkeley: University of California Press.

———. 1991. *Modernity and self-identity: Self and society in the late modern age.* Stanford: Stanford University Press.

Giroux, H. 1983. *Theory and resistance in education: A pedagogy for the opposition.* Massachusetts: Bergin and Garvey.

———. 1994. Living dangerously: Identity politics and the new cultural racism. In *Between borders: Pedagogy and the politics of cultural studies,* ed. H. Giroux and P. McLaren. New York: Routledge.

Goodall, H. L. 1994. *Casing a promised land: The autobiography of an organizational detective as cultural ethnographer.* Carbondale: Southern Illinois University Press.

Graves, R. Forthcoming. Negotiating discourses: Reading, writing, social engagement, and social changes. In *In-siting literacy: Community discourses and teaching composition as social action,* ed. M. Kells, V. Balester, and V. Villanueva.

Grossberg, L. 1994. Introduction: Bringin' it all back home (pedagogy and cultural studies). In *Between borders: Pedagogy and the politics of cultural studies,* ed. H. Giroux and P. McLaren. New York: Routledge.

Guba, E. 1996. Foreword to *Action research: A handbook for practitioners,* by E. Stringer. Thousand Oaks, CA: Sage.

Hall, S., and D. Held. 1990. Citizens and citizenship. In *The changing face of politics in the 1990s,* ed. S. Hall and M. Jacques. London: Verso.

Hammer, M., and J. Champy. 1993. *Reengineering the corporation: A manifesto for business revolution.* New York: HarperBusiness.

Hammer, M., and S. Stanton. 1995. *The reengineering revolution: A handbook.* New York: HarperBusiness.

Hanna, D. E., and Associates. 2000. *Higher education in an era of digital competition: Choices and challenges.* Madison, WI: Atwood.

Hatch, G. 1996. *Arguing in communities.* Mountain View, CA: Mayfield.

Heath, R. 1994. *Management of corporate communication: From interpersonal contacts to external affairs.* Hillsdale, NJ: Lawrence Erlbaum.

Herndl, C., and C. Nahrwold. 2000. Research as social practice: A case study of research on technical and professional communication. *Written Communication* 17 (2): 258–96.

Horton, M. 1990. *The long haul: An autobiography.* Toronto: Doubleday.

Horton, M., and P. Freire. 1990. *We make the road by walking: Conversations on education and social change.* Philadelphia: Temple University Press.

Huckin, T. 1997. Technical writing and community service. *Journal of Business and Technical Communication* 11 (1): 49–59.

Hyman, M. 1995. *PC roadkill.* Foster City, CA: IDG Books.

Jameson, D. A. 2000. Telling the investment story: A narrative analysis of shareholder reports. *Journal of Business Communication* 37 (1): 7–38.

Johansen, R., and R. Swigart. 1994. *Upsizing the individual in the downsized organization: Managing in the wake of reengineering, globalization, and overwhelming technological change.* Reading, MA: Addison-Wesley.

Johnson-Eilola, J. 1996. Relocating the value of work: Technical communications in a post-industrial age. *Technical Communication Quarterly* 5 (3): 245–70.

Kerby, A. 1991. *Narrative and the self.* Bloomington: Indiana University Press.

Lewis, R., and D. Smith. 1994. *Total quality in higher education.* Delray Beach, FL: St. Lucie Press.

Macey, D. 1993. *The lives of Michel Foucault.* New York: Pantheon.

Maturana, H. R., and F. J. Varela. 1980. *Autopoiesis and cognition: The realization of the living.* Dordrecht, Neth.: Reidel.

McMurtry, L. 1999. *Walter Benjamin at the Dairy Queen: Reflections at sixty and beyond.* New York: Simon and Schuster.

Meister, J. 1998. *Corporate universities: Lessons in building a world-class work force.* New York: McGraw-Hill.

Mitford, J. 1963. *The American way of death.* New York: Simon and Schuster.

———. 1997. Death incorporated. *Vanity Fair,* March, 110–31.

———. 2000. *The American way of death revisited.* New York: Vintage Books.

Moore, M. 1987. Ethical discourse and Foucault's conception of ethics. *Human Studies* 10: 81–95.

Moore, T. 1997. The corporate university: Transforming management education. *Accounting Horizons* 11: 77–85.

Morgan, G. 1986. *Images of organization.* Beverly Hills, CA: Sage.

Mumby, D. 1987. The political function of narrative in organizations. *Communication Monographs* 54: 113–27.

———. 1988. *Communication and power in organizations: Discourse, ideology, and domination.* Norwood, NJ: Ablex.

———, ed. 1993. *Narrative and social control: Critical perspectives.* Newbury Park, CA: Sage.

Peters, T. 1992. *Liberation management: Necessary disorganization for the nanosecond nineties.* New York: Fawcett.

Postone, M., E. LiPuma, and C. Calhoun. 1993. Introduction: Bourdieu and social theory. In *Bourdieu: Critical perspectives,* ed. C. Calhoun, E. LiPuma, and M. Postone. Chicago: University of Chicago Press.

Putnum, R. 2000. *Bowling alone: The collapse and revival of American community.* New York: Simon and Schuster.

Reich, R. 1992. *The work of nations.* New York: Vintage.

Rogers, D. 1993. *The future of American banking: Managing for change.* New York: McGraw-Hill.

Rose, P. 1987. *The changing structure of American banking.* New York: Columbia University Press.

Rosenblatt, R. 1999. Millennium essay. *The News Hour with Jim Lehrer,* Public Broadcasting System, December 31.

Rottenberg, A. 1994. *Elements of argument.* Boston: Bedford Books.

Scheper-Hughes, N. 1992. *Death without weeping: The violence of everyday life in Brazil.* Berkeley: University of California Press.

Schwandt, T. 1994. Constructivist, interpretivist approaches to human inquiry. In *Handbook of Qualitative Research,* ed. N. K. Denzen and Y. S. Lincoln. Thousand Oaks, CA: Sage.

Segal, J., A. Paré, D. Brent, and D. Vipond. 1998. The researcher as missionary: Problems with rhetoric and reform in the disciplines. *College Composition and Communication* 50: 71–90.

Selfe, C., and R. Selfe. 1996. Writing as democratic social action in a technological world: Politicizing and inhabiting virtual landscapes. In *Nonacademic writing: Social theory and technology,* ed. A. H. Duin and C. J. Hansen. Mahwah, NJ: Erlbaum.

Senge, P. 1990. *The fifth discipline: The art and practice of the learning organization.* New York: Doubleday.

Simons, J. 1995. *Foucault and the political.* New York: Routledge.

Spellmeyer, K. 1993. *Common ground: Dialogue, understanding, and the teaching of composition.* Englewood Cliffs, NJ: Prentice Hall.

Spilka, R., ed. 1993. *Writing in the workplace: New research perspectives.* Carbondale: Southern Illinois University Press.

Stringer, E. 1996. *Action research: A handbook for practitioners.* Thousand Oaks, CA: Sage.

Sullivan, F. 1997. Dysfunctional workers, functional texts: The transformation of work in institutional procedure manuals. *Written Communication* 14 (3): 313–59.

Sullivan, P., and J. Porter. 1997. *Opening spaces: Writing technologies and critical research practices.* Greenwich, CT: Ablex.

Sumara, D., and T. Carson. 1997. Reconceptualizing action research as a living practice. In *Action research as a living practice,* ed. T. Carson and D. Sumara. New York: Peter Lang.

Tomasko, R. M. 1987. *Downsizing: Reshaping the corporation for the future.* New York: AMACOM.

———. 1993. *Rethinking the corporation: The architecture of change.* New York: AMACOM.

———. 1996. *Go for growth!: Five paths to profit and success—choose the right one for you and your company.* New York: John Wiley and Sons.

Turner, B. A. 1971. *Exploring the industrial subculture.* New York: Seabury.

Van Maanen, J. 1988. *Tales of the field: On writing ethnography.* Chicago: University of Chicago Press.

Willis, P. 1977. *Learning to labor: How working class kids get working class jobs.* New York: Columbia University Press.

Winsor, D. 1989. An engineer's writing and the corporate construction of knowledge. *Written Communication* 6 (3): 270–85.

INDEX

Brenton D. Faber is an assistant professor of technical communications at Clarkson University. He has written extensively on the topics of organizational change, corporate ethics, and academic writing. His consulting work focuses on organizational learning and on nonprofit organizations dealing with change.